THE FACE OF CHRIST IN THE OLD TESTAMENT

THE FACE OF CHRIST IN THE OLD TESTAMENT

GEORGES A. BARROIS

ST. VLADIMIR'S SEMINARY PRESS
1974

TO AUVIAN, BERTRAND, AND RUTH KAY

Table of Contents

Foreword

This book is not an "Introduction to the Old Testament" in the usual sense. Introductions rightly insist on philological information, as a necessary basis for the theological interpretation of the sacred text. But mere erudition should not be an end in itself. The end is Christ, and our objective is to show how the reading of the Old Testament in the light of Tradition leads us to him in whom the Law and the Prophets were fulfilled.

To general readers, we would recommend as study Bibles in English the so-called *Jerusalem Bible,* New York, 1966, or the *Oxford Annotated Bible with the Apocrypha,* New York, 1965, which uses the text of the *Revised Standard Version* (RSV). Both are copiously annotated and provide valuable introductory sections and tables.

We have quoted eclectically from one or another of the available English versions, or we have given our own translations from the Hebrew or Greek originals. The numbering of the Psalms reproduces that of the Hebrew Bible; this has become standard practice; most study Bibles indicate within parentheses or in footnotes the correspondance of the Hebrew notation with the Septuagint (LXX) or the Latin Vulgate. The division of chapters and verses is given according to the *King James* (KJ) and the *Revised Standard Version* (RSV). Slight variations may be expected according to the text, version, or modern translation used by the

readers; cases presenting special difficulties will be noted
when advisable.

Here is an alphabetical list of all the books of the Bible,
with the abbreviations used for reference:

Acts of the Apostles	Acts	Jude	Jude
Amos	Amos	Judges	Jdg
Baruch	Bar	Judith	Jdt
1 Chronicles	1 Chr	1 Kings	1 Ki
2 Chronicles	2 Chr	2 Kings	2 Ki
Colossians	Col	Lamentations	Lam
1 Corinthians	1 Cor	Leviticus	Lev
2 Corinthians	2 Cor	Luke	Lk
Daniel	Dan	1 Maccabees	1 Mac
Deuteronomy	Deut	2 Maccabees	2 Mac
Ecclesiastes (Qoheleth)	Eccle	Malachi	Mal
Ecclesiasticus (Sirach)	Eccli	Mark	Mk
Ephesians	Eph	Matthew	Mt
Esther	Esth	Micah	Mic
Exodus	Ex	Nahum	Nah
Ezekiel	Ezek	Nehemiah	Neh
Ezra	Ezra	Numbers	Num
Galatians	Gal	Obadiah	Obad
Genesis	Gen	1 Peter	1 Pet
Habakkuk	Hab	2 Peter	2 Pet
Haggai	Hag	Philemon	Philem
Hebrews	Heb	Philippians	Phil
Hosea	Hos	Proverbs	Prov
Isaiah	Is	Psalms	Ps
James	Jas	Revelation	Rev
Jeremiah	Jer	Romans	Rom
Job	Job	Ruth	Ruth
Joel	Joel	1 Samuel	1 Sam
John	Joh	2 Samuel	2 Sam
1 John	1 Joh	Song of Songs	S of S
2 John	2 Joh	1 Thessalonians	1 Thes
3 John	3 Joh	2 Thessalonians	2 Thes
Jonah	Jon	1 Timothy	1 Tim
Joshua	Jos	2 Timothy	2 Tim

Titus	Tit	Zechariah	Zech
Tobit	Tob	Zephaniah	Zeph
Wisdom of Solomon	Wis		

References to patristic texts (quoted in our translation, unless noted otherwise) are given according to Migne, *Patrologia Graeca* or *Patrologia Latina,* respectively PG and PL.

For consultation, we would recommend the following atlases and commentaries: *The Biblical Jerome Commentary* (2 volumes in one), Englewood Cliffs, N. J., 1968. *The Interpreter's One-volume Commentary on the Bible,* New York, 1971. More detailed information in *The Anchor Bible,* New York, publication of which began in 1964. *The Westminster Historical Atlas to the Bible* (revised edition), Philadelphia, 1956. L. H. Grollenberg, *Atlas of the Bible,* London, 1956.

Dictionaries: *The Interpreter's Dictionary of the Bible* (4 volumes), New York, 1962. *The Westminster Dictionary of the Bible* (one volume), revised and rewritten by Henry S. Gehman, Philadelphia, 1944.

Aids for further study: Bernhard Anderson, *Understanding the Old Testament,* Englewood Cliffs, N. J., 1966. John Bright, *A History of Israel,* Philadelphia, 1959. Roland de Vaux, *Ancient Israel: Its Life and Institutions* (McGraw-Hill paperback, 2 volumes), New York, 1965. L. H. Grollenberg, *A New Look at an Old Book,* Paramus, N. J., 1969. Artur Weiser, *The Old Testament: Its Formation and Development,* New York, 1961.

CHAPTER I

Reading from the Old Testament

It sounds like a paradox that we should read from the Old Testament in order to discover in it the face of Christ, and in a sense it is. But paradox is of the essence of the Christian mystery: the Increate, breaking into the creative act; the Infinite, giving number and measure to a finite world; the Timeless, yielding to the rhythm of days; the Divine, entering the family of men. The Book of Revelation teaches us that Christ shall be the Last. This demands that we recognize him as the First, for he is the eternal Word by whom all things were made "in the beginning." And it is no mere coincidence that these three words are read in the first verse of Genesis, and in the first verse of the Gospel according to St. John. We reckon by years before Christ, B.C., and years of the Lord, A.D.; the years under the Law, and the years of grace; the Old Testament, and the New Testament. But the Incarnation is more than a serviceable time-divider. The light of the star which rose over Bethlehem is the same light that did shine through darkness on the first day of creation, unto the first man on earth, the fathers of the Old Law and the Gentiles, "every man coming into the world." We have no right to curtail the total perspective of God's revelation. We have been taught to behold the image of Christ in the luminous pages of the Gospel, but we are not therefore to neglect or to despise the rays which have guided the forefathers and sustained their hope. It is always his face we should recognize, glowing amidst the shadows of the remotest past, and his voice we should hear in the reading of the sacred page, in Moses or in the prophets, as well as in the Gospels or in the apostolic writings.

For we should not imagine the divine revelation to be like a flash of lightning which, for a fraction of a second, brings out the minute details of a nocturnal landscape with almost unbearable sharpness, but rather as the gradual unveiling of the mystery under a steadily growing light. The progress of divine revelation is neither uniform nor arbitrary; it does not go by leaps and bounds; the economy of the Providence accommodates itself, by an admirable condescension, to the highs and lows of the human predicament. The incarnation of the Word marks in fact the last stage of a development of which the Old Testament constitutes the authentic record, but God had manifested himself from the beginning "at sundry times and in divers manners" (Heb. 1:1), so as never to leave mankind without a witness. The condition for receiving this witness, however, is that we should be both humble and industrious, failing which I am afraid that we would not benefit much more from the reading of the New Testament.

The first question we must now ask is bluntly this: Do we, Orthodox Christians, read from the Scriptures, and read as we ought to read? I am afraid that we fail on both counts and, worse than that, we are prompt to find cheap excuses to our carelessness. Not so the early Christians. Their extreme reverence for the Sacred Scriptures manifested itself in a number of private devotional acts. It is said of St. Caecilia, a Roman martyr of the early third Christian century, who suffered under Alexander Severus and was buried by order of Pope Urban in the catacomb of St. Callistus, that she used to carry on her breast a miniature Gospel Book.[1] We are reminded of the Jews with their phylacteries on which were written the words of the *Shema':* "Hear O Israel, the Lord our God is one God, and thou shalt love the Lord thy God with all thy heart.... You shall bind these words for a sign upon your hand, and they shall be as frontlets between your eyes" (Deut 6:4-8).

Scripture reading was recommended to all Christians by the Fathers of the Church, who were prompt in denouncing their charges' negligence. St. John Chrysostom upbraided the Christians of his time who would excuse themselves on account of their many occupations, as busy Americans are wont to do.

> Do not give me of that shabby nonsense: "I am tied up in court business, enmeshed in public affairs, involved in the pursuit of my art; I have a wife, children to feed, I must provide for my household; I am just an ordinary man. To read the Scriptures is not for me, but for those who have renounced the world." Man, what are you saying there? It is for you, even more than for them. Tossed as we are on the high seas, pressed by ten thousand hazards, we need, willy-nilly, the comfort of the Scriptures.[2]

Note here that it is the private reading, at home, which is recommended in this passage of Chrysostom, and this "not only to all men, but to women as well."[3] Toward the same time, St. Jerome outlined a program of study for a little girl, seven years old, the age of discretion. She would learn the Psalter by rote, and "make the Books of Solomon, the Gospels, the Apostles and the Prophets the treasure of her heart."[4] Writing to a young widow, he advised her to persevere in frequent prayer and in Scripture reading, the *lectio divina,* declared to be an excellent remedy against the subconscious movements of the passions.[5]

In sharp contrast with the encouragements given to the faithful and with the "Open Bible" policy of the patristic era, restrictive measures were taken by the western mediaeval Church as a protection against heretical sects and lay movements escaping hierarchical control. The sixteenth-century split within western Christianity aggravated the situation still further and resulted on the part of Rome in a tightening of the rules relative to the diffusion or teaching of the Scriptures, to the translation of the original texts or ancient versions into vernacular, and to the reading of the Bible by the laity. The majority of the faithful had to be satisfied with hearing the liturgical sections of the Gospels and of the Epistles being chanted at Mass, and commented—sometimes—in the pulpit. Few were the Catholic homes in which a vernacular edition of the New Testament could be found, and fewer still of the Old Testament. Now this does not mean conversely that there is a Bible in every modern Jewish or Protestant home; furthermore the mere possession of a family Bible is no proof that it is perused regularly outside of solemn circumstances. The starvation diet to which the Roman Catholic laity had been subjected for so long was gradually lifted during the first two decades of this century, when the revival of Biblical studies in institutions of clerical learning began to reach the mass of the faithful. The progress, however, was greatly slowed down in intellectual circles by the modernist crisis and hampered among lay people by the inroads of secularism.

As might be expected, Scripture reading among the Protestants has remained a standard practice, at least in theory. Unfortunately the negative attitude taken regarding Tradition has left Protestantism defenseless against the pressure of passing ideologies and the secularization of modern culture. Hence a gamut of theological systems evincing or succeeding one another, while paradoxically appealing to the authority of Scripture. It is difficult to see how this diversity of orientations can possibly result in the formulation of workable guidelines for the theological understanding of the Biblical message by lay people.

This leaves to us the task of listening to the Word of God in the ambiance provided by the Church, in the peace of the sanctuary, where the voice that spake of old can still be heard. The sad fact, however, is that thus far the attitude of the Orthodox toward the Bible leaves much to be desired. A vigorous renewal is urgently needed, on the basis of the authentic tradition of the Church. Writes Fr. Alexander

Schmemann: "Orthodox theology has never felt at home in modern Biblical scholarship and has not accepted as its own the Biblical problems as formulated within the western theological development. . . . One can predict that a revival will consist, first of all, of a deep reassessment and re-evaluation of western biblicism."[6]

The standard excuse for neglecting the Old Testament is that "It is old; so, why bother with it? The New suffices; the Old has become obsolete, irrelevant." I use this second adjective intentionally, because it is a favorite in the word-list of young Americans who, by a marvelous inconsequence, comb the flea-markets for antiques.

Of course, such a rationalization is specious. There are in the Old Testament, its temporal and special conditioning, elements which are totally foreign to the mentality of twentieth-century men and women, be they Americans, Eurasians, Africans or Orientals. We would expect modern Judaism to be homogeneous with the Old Testament; indeed it is, to a measure. Yet the evolutive process of which it constitutes the present stage and which has been going on for centuries has taken its toll and left the historical field littered with lifeless remains from the past. The early tribal-national cradle of the Hebrew people fell apart in the sixth century B.C.; the early prophetic writings had already denounced the people's blind trust in a covenant of which they fulfilled not the obligations, and the post-exilic prophets looked farther and higher for the realization of Israel's hope; the Temple, deemed to be indestructible, was destroyed and desecrated three times, the Wailing Wall alone subsists today, a relic or a "place of interest" for the tourists; the synagogal institution was forced on the people by the necessity to survive in the Diaspora as a religious community; Zionism emerges as a secular, economic, socio-cultural phenomenon, more than a revival of the ancient alliance. Something died at each of these successive transformations. There is no denying that the Old Testament has been superseded in at least some of its transitory, provisional features; but to declare it worthless or maybe harmful would be a fatal *non sequitur.* It remains an essential organ of God's self-disclosure and it has its message for today and for the days to come.

We should refrain from quoting out of context such sentences of the Sermon on the Mount as: "You have heard that it was said . . . but I say unto you. . ." (Mt 5:21 ff). Text for text, let us rather hear the formal statement of Our Lord: "Think not that I am come to destroy the Law and the Prophets . . . for verily I say unto you: Till heaven and earth pass, one jot or one tittle shall in no wise pass from the Law, till all be fulfilled" (Mt 5:17).

The trouble is, we read superficially; we absolutize transitory features, and we find irreducible opposition where there should be harmonious synthesis. We forget that the written Word is in itself an incarnational reality and, if we be permitted to apply to the Old and the New Testament the terminology of the Fourth Ecumenical Council, we would say that they are to be kept without confusion, mutation, division, nor separation.

We have no right to oppose the Old Testament to the New, or to choose from either that which appeals to us, and by-pass, neglect or reject the rest, through caprice, or following an attempt at rationalizing our choice on the basis of a preconceived ideology. This would be properly heresy (αἵρεσις), and there have been heretics all along the history of revelation. Samaritans read exclusively the Pentateuch, a heresy by ignorance originating in a defective indoctrination. The Karaïtes professed Biblical purism to the exclusion of rabbinical tradition—from a Jewish standpoint, a formal heresy. St. Paul had denounced the rise of heretical cliques among the Christians of his time. A century later, a heretical movement threatened to warp irremediably the very texture of Christianity: toward the middle of the second century, a Christian from Asia Minor, Marcion, contrasted the Old and the New Testament in support of his antisemitic bias and of his (justifiable) opposition to groups of Judaizers, heirs to those who had given so much trouble to the Apostle. Marcion claimed that there is an irreducible contradiction between the Old Testament Creator, the jealous God of the Jews, and the God of love who manifested himself first in Christ.[7] Toward the middle of the fourth century, the radical dualism of the Manichaeans swept through the Christian world, offering a pseudo-metaphysical theory for a fundamental reinterpretation of Christianity. The opposition between the world of matter, work of a demiurge, and the world of the spirit, God's world, was seen by them as absolute; there was no reconciling two eternally hostile principles. Repeatedly condemned by the entire hierarchy, their ideology lived on under a variety of names and aliases during the Middle Ages.[8] Working from their axiomatic dualism, they repudiated the Old Testament, sorted out that which could be salvaged or reinterpreted according to their doctrine, and weeded out of the New Testament whatever they suspected of compromission with the Old Testament or contamination by impure contacts.

I am conscious of having ranged far beyond the limits of my object. The excursus, however, may convince us of the necessity of aiming at a grasp of the Scriptures in their totality, as the privileged organ and vehicle of divine revelation. Differences of tonality and perspective between the Old and the New Testament should not induce us into operating a disjunction; we should rather learn to read them in their complementarity, short of which our understanding of either one is bound to remain unilaterally biased. Since we hold the Scriptures to be an authentic record of the divine revelation, running from Genesis to the Apocalypse, it is imperative that we should scrutinize each phase of the revelational process if we are to feel the full impact of the Gospel. This is not a matter of choice. There is only one revelation under two successive dispensations of the same divine condescendence toward men; not as if God, realizing the failure of his original design, had decided upon a new approach to save sinners, but because, having created man in his likeness, he would call him to share in the divine blessedness. Thus was God's eternally begotten son born a man, in order that men would be "capable of the divinity" (δεκτικὸν θεό-τητος).[9]

If positive reasons are wanted to induce Christians into reading the Old Testament, I can think immediately of the following: first, the Old Testament has been the Book which the Lord Jesus learned as a child, read as a man, and lay open before his disciples, in his teaching and in his life. The first episode coming to mind is when he got lost in the throng of the Passover pilgrims in Jerusalem and was found by Joseph and Mary in a hall of the Temple, "sitting in the midst of the masters, listening to them and asking questions from them" (Lk 2: 46); questions about what?—Obviously about the Law or the Prophets, the written Word, which they were reading and interpreting. St. Luke adds that the bystanders were much impressed by the intelligence of his answers and concludes by saying that Jesus "grew in wisdom, age, and grace before God and men" (Lk 2:47, 52). This "asking questions" and "growing in wisdom" seems to have puzzled some early Church writers who felt, like Clement of Alexandria, "that no one being greater than the Logos, no one therefore can be a master to Him who alone is the Master."[10] The difficulty is real; we hit again upon the basic paradox of the Incarnation. As God, Jesus Christ knew all things; as a man, during his life on earth, he was subject to the human mode of acquiring knowledge. Had he not learned to read, as a child? Perhaps from his mother, as it was suggested by the *locorum monstratores,* worthy predecessors of the modern guides of Jerusalem, who unhesitatingly did show to gullible pilgrims the house where the Theotokos had "learned the letters." The balanced formulae of the definition of Chalcedon "according to divinity . . . according to humanity. . ." are theologically unassailable, but the problem remains unsolved.[11] Any attempt at figuring out what can have been the psychology of him who was both God and man is, a priori, doomed to failure; but what we should realize here is that the Incarnate Word, when he heard the Law being read by the doctors, was in fact listening to his own voice, to the words he had uttered, to the deeds he had ordered, to the wonders he had wrought, as the eternal Logos of the eternal Father.

Some twenty years after the "Invention in the Temple,"

a young carpenter entered the synagogue of Nazareth on a sabbath day, "and he stood up to read, and there was given to him the book of the prophet Isaiah. He opened the book and found the place where it is written, 'The Spirit of the Lord is upon me, because he has anointed me to preach good news to the poor. He has sent me to proclaim release to the captives and recovering of sight to the blind, to set at liberty those who are oppressed, to proclaim the acceptable year of the Lord.' And he closed the book, and gave it back to the attendant and the eyes of all in the synagogue were fixed on him. And he began to say to them, 'Today this Scripture has been fulfilled in your hearing.' " (Lk 4:16-21, quoting Is 61:1-2). We may reasonably assume that the inspired words of the prophets formed the very program of Christ's preaching in the synagogues of Galilee during the years of his public life, a teaching received with a mixture of wonder and suspicion on the part of his auditors; was he a "blue-collar worker" or a "miraculous rabbi"?

Again, on the evening after the Resurrection, it is the point-by-point exposition of the Scriptures which constituted the essence of the catechesis to the disciples of Emmaus, when the Risen Lord, "beginning at Moses and all the Prophets, interpreted to them in all the Scriptures the things concerning himself," thus unveiling the entire economy of salvation (Lk 24:27). We should not need anything more than these three episodes to be convinced that we may confidently seek the face of our Christ in the Old Testament as in a magic mirror. The prophets did speak, but it is, of a truth, the voice of Christ we hear.

This was self-evident to the Fathers of the Church and the early ecclesiastical writers, regardless of their technique of interpretation, whether, like Origen and a majority of Greek and Latin authors, they used the allegorical method for probing and expounding the hidden depths of the Scriptures, or felt it safer to rely on the historical substratum of the revelation, like the Antiochians and their followers. By and large, the latter approach is generally preferred today, as being more "scientific"—it is also more pedestrian! At any rate, an informed and competent study of the letter of the sacred page, both of the Old and of the New Testament, is indispensable as a first step toward total interpretation.

St. Jerome had felt the need of studying the Scriptures of the Old Testament according to the best readings of the Hebrew text. He tells of his heroic efforts at learning a language which he disliked for its structure, its "hissing sounds" and its "throat-flaying gutturals";[12] he hired Jewish tutors at great personal expense,[13] and was not a little proud of his achievements when, ironically, he boasted: "I am a philosopher, rhetor, grammarian, dialectician; also trilingual to boot: Hebrew, Greek, and Roman."[14]

The tradition of the Evangelists and of the Apostles, and the tradition of the Fathers merge into the liturgical tradition of the Church. They form a trilogy which should be a powerful incentive to our reading of the Old Testament, the common source from which they draw abundantly. A mere glance at our liturgical books and, still better, our attendance or participation in the services of our church, would make us realize how dense is the Old Testament atmosphere in which we breathe and live. The same can be said of the liturgical treasury of the Latin Church, whether we open a Missal or a Breviary.[15] The cycle of readings throughout the Christian year, distributed according to the proper genius of the Latin or of the Byzantine rite, confronts us with the entire history of salvation. In the Latin Breviaries, the Old Testament lessons for Matins and the corresponding *responsoria* prescribed for the various seasons of the year are designated appropriately in the rubrics as the "dominical history" (*historia dominicalis*). Our Byzantine *troparia* and *kontakia,* the poetry of our hymnographs, would be unintelligible without a modicum of acquaintance with the Old Testament, and it is the historical revelation of grace, from Moses to the opening chapters of St. Luke's Gospel, which provided the basic theme of the canons which are sung at the *Orthros.*

Some may fear that this preponderance of Old Testament material can mute for us the call of the present hour, by making us play a sterile game of archaeology. Not at all! It means rather that, seeing the projection of the face of

Christ through the optics of the Old Testament, we may turn to him, "reaching forth unto those things which lie ahead" (Phil 3:13), where our expectation shall resolve into the final integration of the mystical body. Let this, from now on, be our constant objective.

CHAPTER II

Preparation to the Gospel

There seems to be in our days a renewal of interest in the Bible, in various circles and for various motives. A statistical analysis might be instructive, but we are not competent to undertake it, and it would take us far beyond the limits of this essay. Let it suffice to point to announcements advertizing the Bible as "still a best-seller," and the popularity of college courses on "the Bible as literature," or the listing of the Bible in a curriculum based on the "Great Books."

The trouble is that our contemporaries, literate though they are supposed to be, have forgotten how to read. Methods of fast reading, abundantly advertized through the media, may be helpful for locating a passage in a hurry, but running a marathon through the dense pages of the Bible, Old Testament, New Testament and Apocrypha, will only wear out our eyes and leave us intellectually and spiritually starved.

The essential requirement for Scripture reading, as well as for praying, is that both mind and heart should apply themselves to whatever is voiced, or heard, or sung.[1] It is not immaterial that a number of Psalms are entitled in Hebrew *maskîl,* meaning a didactic poem, and we are exhorted to sing "wisely," ψάλατε συνετῶς, *psallite sapienter, erudite* (Ps 47:6).

It is a matter of common experience that the Word, read or chanted at the lectern or from the ambon of our churches, has a soul-grasping virtue of its own, as if harmonies were awakened, which we would not perceive otherwise. St. Augustine confessed, with the rhetorical pathos customary of him, how deeply he had been moved by the antiphonal singing recently introduced in the western Church by St. Ambrose of Milan: "The voices flowed in my ears, and the truth was poured forth into my heart, whence the tide of my devotion overflowed, and my tears ran down."[2] One thing is to read the Lamentations of Jeremiah "in the closet," another thing is to let ourselves be carried away by their mournful melody during Holy Week, in a Latin Church. One thing is to read privately the Canon of St. Andrew of Crete, another thing is to hear it being solemnly chanted during Great Lent, and to conclude each stasis with an ardent appeal for mercy. It all requires, of course, that priests, deacons, readers, the choir and the faithful, apply themselves in earnest to their office, and do not dispatch it like that reader in Pasternak's *Doctor Zhivago,* who went "rattling away the Beatitudes at a speed which suggested that they were well enough known without him."

The message of the Bible is being received, so to speak, on different wave-lengths. From a mere aesthetic point of view, the craving of nineteenth-century artists and poets for the picturesque, the exotic and the esoteric, is perhaps on the wane. We are not much impressed any more by the mere consonance of Hebrew words, as was Victor Hugo, who even invented some for the sake of the rhyme. Yet, movie producers and authors of cheap thrillers still fare on the "couleur locale" of Bible stories.

It is generally agreed that the Bible could and should play an important role in modern education. Especially archaeological researches and discoveries in the Bible lands have become part of general scholarship and also a fashionable parlor topic, in connection with the wholesale awakening of the Near and Middle East, and recent events in those lands. Information about the Bible, ever so rudimentary, is therefore considered as a useful, even indispensable, element of modern culture. Unfortunately, the common trend, rarely opposed, is toward neutralism in matter of religion. Were it not for what derives properly from the Gospel, the program of many a Sunday School could be run equally well in a Reformed synagogue. Doctrinal values receive little or no attention, because doctrine is seen as a cause of division among Christians. Our contemporaries shun rather than seek precision on religious topics because they fear to appear different from their neighbors, or because they feel that doctrine is not necessary for living as a good Christian or a good citizen. We would be the last to deprecate the positive aspects of their Scripture-inspired moralism, even though it be a-doctrinal, but we cannot defend ourselves from feeling that, apart from a few notable exceptions, a "modernized" Christianity, for not being rooted any more in the absolute truth of divine revelation, represents a residue which lacks power to regenerate itself in the midst of a secularized culture; it has lost much of its radioactivity.

A number of young people, who apparently care little or not at all for conventional aesthetics or moralistic indoctrination, are apt to blame the mediocrity of our so-called Christian culture on the ecclesiastical establishment; they denounce loudly the faked respectability of their leaders and of their elders, who proclaim lofty principles and fail to live up to them. What these youngsters seek, in the Scriptures or elsewhere, is not a set of moral standards, but a compensation for their unsatisfied mysticism and a guidance for the immediate realization of their not ungenerous, if utopic, desires. The "vibrations," if we may use one of their favorite expressions, are often authentic but, for lack of proper control, result into countercultures, either self-styled Christian, or wildly radical. There may be a lot of Bible reading, unguided and erratic. Attitudes range from Bible Belt literalism to extreme liberalism, from disregard for articulate thinking to deliberate negation of any clear-cut profile in matters of belief, from untested fits of enthusiasm to esoteric ritualism, with perhaps less consistency than may be found among the youthful members of the Hare Krishna sect, who go chanting and proselytizing in Harvard Square or in the New York bus terminal, in obvious reaction against the upbringing which they have received—or failed to receive—in their family. Impressionism or expressionism is not the proper approach to Christian revelation, no matter what the motivation is. We cannot regard the Bible as a mere stimulus to religious thinking and read it to suit our taste. We need objective reasons for setting apart the Bible as unique and demanding our allegiance. There may be other ways than the Biblical way, but the Biblical way cannot be traced on quicksand.

A rigorous historical method is necessary for establishing the study of the Biblical message or, if you wish, of Biblical literature, on firm grounds. Such a necessity derives from the fact that the Bible actually refers to verifiable events which happened in particular places, to nations which appeared, waxed and waned in the course of history, to persons whose activities were recorded, and the records themselves preserved, edited and compiled over a considerable length of time. We are thus presented with a double set of closely related factors: the very substance of all that which is recorded in the Bible, and the manner, the quality and the modalities of the recording itself. It belongs to literary and historical criticism to scrutinize both and to pronounce over their mutual relationship. What is involved here is the historicity of the Bible, a notion deceptively simple in appearance, yet in fact slippery and extremely complex.

Historicity as such may be described, rather than defined, as that particular quality of documents relative to events of the past, situations, physical or psychological facts, inasmuch as the memory of such, at first transmitted by word of mouth, subsequently consigned in writing and eventually gathered into compilations of diverse age, worth, and purpose, forms the subject-matter of history.

It is obvious that the historical enterprise suffers from limitations imputable either to incomplete information, or to the very nature of some particular object, the essence of which is not susceptible of positive measurement. On both counts history will never yield an ironclad demonstration of the Christian event or a cold justification of our beliefs. No human method can possibly result in a grasp of the revelation equal to its object, and our understanding of Scripture, no matter how far it progresses along the pathways of history, will never reach an ever-receding horizon. St. Gregory the Great observes that even the certainty of the sacred language "grows in proportion to the spiritual capacity of the readers."[3]

The historical method as it was conceived and expressed in the course of the nineteenth century, bears the imprint of positivism. The emphasis was on the critical examination of the documents from a formal point of view: textual criticism, age and origin of the sources, identification and credibility of authors, editors and compilers, and the like. It submitted the raw material of history to an acid test, eliminating faked or irrelevant documents and retaining only, so to speak, that which would be "receivable in court."

Such a method guarantees unimpeachable conclusions within its own limits. It suffers, however, from an unjustified minimalism, by making little or no allowance for imponderable quantities resisting any kind of regimentation and not admissible as factual evidence, yet offering precious information to the historian. We cannot afford to overlook psychological factors more difficult to identify, record, or interpret than external facts and events, nor should we leave untapped valuable sources, because they are deemed extraneous or marginal to history strictly understood. We eventually learn more from folklore, popular legends and sayings, than from the most exact, matter-of-fact chronicle.

The rigidity of the positive method gradually has been humanized. Most historians today refuse to be laced in the straitjacket of unworkable rules which had been inspired by ideological considerations rather than by the specific requirements of the discipline. Perceptible regularities of occurrence, which can be statistically ascertained, confront us with a virtually intelligible pattern, with chains of facts and events which cannot be reduced to a mechanistic system of causes and effects. The most sceptical must admit that, beyond the listing of past happenings, history makes at least *some* sense.[4]

Recent developments in the domain of the philosophy of history, incidentally a discipline which was always regarded with suspicion by "pure" historians, show forth a particular interest in the analysis of the notion of causality as applied to historical happenings. This has led Professor Morton White categorically to reject any tentative of a monistic justification for historical occurrences, as would be an all-out mechanistic hypothesis, an all-out economic, or political, or ecological explanation. In his own words, "to adopt a monistic theory of *the* explanation . . . in any branch of history is as indefensible as to adopt one in law. It is much like saying that automobile accidents are always to be explained by reference to the icy condition of the road, or to the drunkenness of the driver, or to faulty brakes."[5] The adjective "historical" is polyvalent; the notion of historicity applies proportionally to the various quantities we call historical and which, in one way or another, are legitimate objects of history. These considerations may, it is hoped, prevent some misunderstandings and help in clarifying what we mean, when we speak of the historicity of the Bible.

As could be expected, the revival of Biblical scholarship from the mid-nineteenth century onward has been conditioned by the parallel development of the historical sciences. The critical method advocated by the early theoricians of history had inspired the efforts of western scholars for revisiting the Bible, especially the Old Testament. Radicals eager to free themselves from confessional ties, rejected or bypassed the claim of the Bible to be an inspired writing and an authentic record of the divine revelation. The Old Testament had to be put in its place as just a piece of eastern literature, and Biblical religion as just one more Semitic religion. Catholic scholars countered by trying to use the critical method constructively in order to buttress, rather than to batter, the traditional positions. A certain apologetic overtone is easily detected in Fr. Lagrange's *La méthode historique,* which met, alas, with suspicion and even hostility on the part of ultra-conservative elements in the Roman curia and in the Church at large.[6] These battles were fought on the terrain of Biblical criticism as such. But criticism is only one part of what we would call "total exegesis"; it is preparatory with regard to the final goal, which is to be reached only through a process of interpretation (the science of hermeneutics) germane to the message conveyed by the text. In conservative circles, Biblical hermeneutics continued to reflect theological formulations having no necessary connection with the Bible text. On the other hand, critically-minded scholars often stopped halfway, being satisfied with the results of their analyses, which enabled them to state what the Bible says, without passing judgment on the implications of what it says. Such attitudes were of course not sufficient for a vigorous revival of Biblical science. This, incidentally, was deplored by excellent scholars who, by reason of life circumstances, had concentrated their efforts on historical criticism.[7] We too believe that the spiritual interpretation of the message, after the mind of the Fathers—this does not mean servile imitation—should be next in order of urgency, as it is indispensable for the edification of the Church.

The record of Biblical scholarship in Orthodoxy is rather scanty, and this may be explained in part by historical circumstances, namely: the isolation and struggle for survival of the Ecumenical Throne, the problems of the Church of Greece in the midst of national reconstruction and the vicissitudes of two world wars and revolutions, the efforts of Russian theology to purge itself of westernizing influences. There are unmistakable signs of recovery and evidence of growth: the pioneering work of Fr. Florovsky, the initiative taken by Orthodox theologians from Saloniki and Athens to investigate systematically the principles of interpretation which the Bible itself suggests and which guided the Church Fathers. A number of Roman scholars are working toward similar objectives, and are to be commended for the publication of such series as *Sources Chrétiennes,* or the more popular American collections.[8]

The problem before us at this point is: how, and to what extent, can the Bible, and particularly the Old Testament, be called historical? More precisely: which items in the sacred page, either directly or indirectly expressed, qualify as *historical* records of the revelation, and from which standpoint can they be ascribed the note of historicity? First of all, the adjective "historical," when it is predicated of the Biblical message, calls for a modifier. The Bible is not whatever kind of history, but sacred history, and this epithet is not adventitious, as the product of some afterthought; it is an essential element of the definition. The Bible claims to have been delivered to men under the seal and guaranty of the Holy Spirit, who inspired the human authors.[9] This claim is stated explicitly in an impressive number of passages diversely worded and endorsed by the Jewish tradition, from all of which it can be inferred that we should regard the whole Book as sacred. The historian, even if he is an unbeliever, has no right to overlook the formal claim of the Old Testament to being the authentic record of the divine revelation, as was acknowledged by the entire tradition. These are historical factors, and to exclude them, ignore them, or make abstraction from them, is a vice of method. They must be accepted as part of the material evidence laid before us, and they demand to be examined sympathetically. This is a minimum requirement.

On the other hand, the fact that we Christians believe in the reality of the revelation does not mean that we regard the Bible as a monolithic monument, of forbidding aspect. Even a superficial glance would make a reader soon aware of its composite nature, as a collection of laws, stories, histories, chronicles, oracles, prayers, lyrics, aphorisms from ancient sages, written, edited and compiled at different periods and by a variety of authors, free and responsible agents working under the invisible motion of God's Spirit.

We have described the notion of historicity as polyvalent. It applies, first, to the traditional divisions of the Bible, and, second, to the original fragments and traditions which were gathered in them. The Hebrew divisions of the Bible— the *Torah* (the Law, contained in the five Books of Moses),

the *Nebi'im* (meaning what we call the historical Books
from Joshua to Kings, plus the Prophets strictly speaking),
the *Ketubim* (the "other" writings)—invite us to a dis-
criminate reading of each section in particular, according to
its function in the religious history of Israel. It is evident
that the narratives of the creation and the origins of mankind, the history of the Patriarchs and of the Hebrew tribes,
the promulgation of the Law, the annals of Israel and
Judah, the impassionate appeal of the Prophets, the plaint
of Job and the disillusioned musings of Ecclesiastes, do not
bear the same relation to the totality of the revelation.
Historicity, as ascribed to those pieces, is a variable. This
does not mean that, as Christians, we are at liberty to distinguish in the Holy Scriptures elements inspired and therefore authoritative, from statements not inspired. The charism
of inspiration is such that everything in Holy Scripture is,
in some way or other, instrumental to the revelation of the
Christian mystery. It remains, however, that not everything
is susceptible to be investigated through an historical inquiry.

It is in the claim of the Scriptures to reveal the economy
of God's dealing with his creatures that the key to the
discovery of a "constant" under the "variables" brought
forth by Biblical criticism is to be discovered. We would
like here to use the German term *Heilsgeschichte,* History
of Salvation, with the proviso that "Salvation" is understood
comprehensively according to the tradition of the Church,
so as to embrace restoration, integration, and recapitulation—
the ἀνακεφαλαίωσις of St. Irenaeus.[10] The historical
synthesis resulting from the application of the above principles
should be the antidote to the disastrous impression of frag-
mentation left on a casual observer by an apparent excess
of critical analysis, and it would show how the stage was
set for the Incarnation of the Word and the proclamation
of the Gospel.

CHAPTER III

The Gospel in the Old Testament

The Old Testament record implies "directionality." It is future-oriented. We read it, so to speak, "downstream." While the headwaters of the stream are inaccessible—so have been, for a long time, the sources of the Nile—the accessible portions of our stream, its main channel and its dormant waters can be charted to a reasonable degree of accuracy. To be sure, the mouth of the stream is still beyond our reach, hidden in an inscrutable future. Nevertheless, the general progression of Biblical history can be traced through the Books of the Old Testament, *as we read them today.*

These last words need underscoring, for the Bible did not fall, ready made, from heaven. Modern criticism does not make it permissible to entertain that kind of illusion any more. We know we have to reckon with miscellaneous traditions, with fragments written at different times and in different places, and gathered into corpora, as are the Books of Moses, the Prophets, the Psalms and the Wisdom writings, the annals of the Hebrew kingdoms, the Temple records, and the documents of the post-exilic restoration. All these have been edited, bound as it were "under stiff cover." Finally, the Hebrew and the Alexandrian canon of Scriptures presented the translators, ancient and modern, with a definitive text to interpret.

The analysis of this process of transmission should not make us lose from sight the organic unity of the Bible as a whole. We believe that it is possible to discern, under the bewildering variety of the original pieces of which the Bible is composed and which eventually diverge from each other, a living Tradition—*T* upper case—the Παράδοσις, underlying the Scriptural record of the Old Testament. It should not be confused with tradition—*t* lower case and generally in the plural—meaning habits of understanding or doing things.

Here we must stress once more, to the risk of sounding repetitious, the gradually developing, dynamic nature of Tradition. It is not the mere passing on of a static "given" once and for all. It pulsates with the progress of revelation; it precedes and follows Scripture; it is never an adjunct, nor an adventitious growth; it gives meaning to the vicissitudes of God's people in Old Testament times, and it is ultimately brought into focus in the Church of Christ. The canon of Scriptures closes when the historical task of the Incarnate Logos is fulfilled on earth. Tradition lives forth in the Church of Pentecost, enlightening the minds and shaping the lives of Christians.

The progressive character of the Biblical revelation is not to be understood as uniform. We have compared its progression to the course of a stream, but the stream of Biblical history does not flow evenly. It has its accidents, eddies, wild stretches and meanders. Its course is continuous in time, for it is always God who continues to reveal himself, but God's self-disclosure is somehow conditioned by the men who are its beneficiaries. The one theme, unchangeable in essence, but developed through the ages, demands successive transpositions, in order to be understood correctly.[1] The messianic theme runs through the entire Bible, but there are three ages of Old Testament messianism. First, the age of the promise to the Fathers, God's blessing upon Abraham and his posterity, the tribes gathered into one nation and established in the land of Canaan. Second, the royal messianism, when the covenant with the Fathers is transposed into God's sworn fidelity to David and his dynasty. The third age is marked by a further transformation of the original theme: the messianic triumph is postponed to the last day of history, in the apocalyptic vision of a new heaven and a new earth. The incarnation of the Son of God brings us back from outer space to our human world, when the Messiah, son of David according to the flesh, inaugurates in his death and resurrection the kingdom which has no end.

The evident growth in explicitation of the divine revelation excludes any conception of history and particularly of salvation history as a succession of happenings having mere episodic value. Such could only be described, but they would offer no basis for a qualitative evaluation, nor for an anticipation of the future, otherwise than by mere guesswork or by statistical projection. The entire weight of Scripture and Tradition supposes a τέλος, a goal, a divinely appointed objective, toward which rational agents, willy-nilly, converge, as well as the entire creation. Moreover, the τέλος, principle of universal attraction, origin of every motion, must be a personal τέλος; he is identified in the Old Testament through his providential intervention in the world of men; he is named in the New Testament, even Jesus Christ, who is the keystone of the entire οἰκονομία. And the New Testament is called New, not just because it comes after the Old, but because it comes as the conclusion of one single plan, already before us, but awaiting consummation. Salvation history involves essentially an anticipation of the latter things, τὰ ἔσχατα; it resolves into an eschatology, not indeed as if the kingdom had been realized, or as if its realization were an otherworldly dream without consistency. The eschatology of the Bible, as Fr. Florovsky felicitously calls it, is an inaugurated eschatology.

Teleology, viz. the theory of final causation, is admittedly the most maligned part of the mediaeval teaching on the four causes, intemperately exploited by late scholasticism. It originates in Aristotle's speculations on the empirical production of material things: the artist envisions an ideal form and applies himself to realizing it in the material of which he disposes; an inform lump of clay, the "matter," ὕλη, is being fashioned into a work of art, the "form" of which, μορφή,[2] corresponds as faithfully as possible to the ideal model which the artist dreamt of as his objective, his τέλος. Thus the work of the artist in his studio is set in motion, so to speak attracted, by his ideal vision. Modern philosophers tend to limit the validity of teleological explanations to cases in which a goal is consciously pursued, or to phenomena suggesting a clear evidence of design. The latter may be observed—and interpreted with due caution—in the domain of biological sciences, where life phenomena, including the adaptation or eventual modification of organs, are manifestly ordained to the preservation of individuals from embryo to adulthood, and to the perpetuation of the species.

Contrary to what could be expected, it is the scientists, rather than the philosophers, who are the least inclined to give up teleology as a valid element of causal explanation, and who are interested in clarifying the conditions of its applicability. While admitting that the hypothesis "God" was not needed for formulating his equations, Einstein just could not believe that God was playing dice with the universe.[3] The indefatigable efforts of the late Fr. Teilhard de Chardin for the integration of Christian faith within the evolution of the Universe involved an axiomatic acceptance of teleology. Teilhard, who had little taste for the categories of scholasticism and their derivatives, conceived the evolution of the cosmos from primordial inertia, through developmental stages overlapping at times, "anthropogenesis," "cosmogenesis," "Christogenesis," unto the "pleromization" at the "Omega point," where the tension of mind and matter would be resolved, and where the "cosmic Christ" would be all in all. Everything in his system[4] postulates an ultimate goal, which alone gives a meaning to the developments of nature. Teilhard was criticized and accused of pantheism, confusion of orders, materialistic monism or personification of the cosmos, universalism, an insufficient doctrine on sin and a defective Christology, through neglect of scriptural or traditional data. The charges, merciless, may not be totally unjustified; the fact is that Teilhard's incurable romanticism and a terminology of his own invention does not make easy the task of those who undertake his defense.

Teleological explanations in historical disciplines ought to be formulated with utter care, all the more in the history of salvation, since God's energy is immediately involved here; no human analogy, therefore, can validly apply, but only the analogy of faith.

Mediaeval philosophy used to express the reciprocal relationship between the effective cause and the final cause by the following adage: *primum in intentione, ultimum in executione,* "that which is first in the order of intention, comes last in the order of execution." The reciprocity of the two orders, however, does not mean that it should be possible, starting from where we stand, to retrace inerringly the mechanism of history, which depends on free agents, confronted with an infinite number of options. Yet it might be possible, in a general way and at our own risk, to work our way backwards. We would direct the beam of light through the twilight of the past ages, which were never in complete darkness, and, instead of drifting down the course of Biblical history, we would, so to speak, paddle upstream. Vistas already known to us would appear in a different perspective; light effects would change; features of which we had caught only a glimpse while floating down the river, would retain our attention; we would meet at each turn with a mixture of newness and of "already seen," and yet it would be the same river and the same revelation. Reading the Bible from the vantage point of the Christian mystery, the Passion, the Resurrection, the effusion of the Spirit at Pentecost, may not teach us more things about Christ himself, but it will increase our understanding of what we know of him.

For the early Christians, the Jewish Scriptures were the

only record of the revelation. The leaders of the Church were careful to authenticate their profession of faith by calling on the witness of the Old Testament. Hence, in the Gospel narratives, especially in Matthew, Mark, and John, to a lesser degree in Luke, the recurrence of such formulae as: "All of this was done, that (ἵνα) it might be fulfilled which was spoken by the prophet" (Mt 1:22); "for thus (οὕτως γάρ) it is written by the prophet" (Mt 2:5); "then was fulfilled (τότε ἐπληρώθη) that which was spoken by Jeremy" (Mt 2:17); "for this is he that was spoken of by the prophet" (Mt 3:3), or similar clauses.

The above examples were taken from the initial chapters of the first Gospel, but the same observations could be made on the basis of the other New Testament writings. We admit that the accumulation of these stereotyped formulae may appear suspicious. Yet they are something more than a mere literary device. The Gospel writers and the Gospel preachers of the first Christian generation made use of them, perhaps too lavishly for our own taste, because they expressed their preoccupations, as they were anxious to watch the signs of the times. The problem has been thoroughly discussed by the theoricians of form criticism (*Formgeschichte*).[5] We need not be alarmed at the use of the conjunction ἵνα, "in order that," to express the relationship between Gospel events and the prophecies of the Old Testament.[6] The point which the Evangelists wish to make is that the economy of the Old Testament finds its achievement in the New.

This, of course, is for us of the utmost importance. It means nothing less than this: by applying ourselves to the reading of the Old Testament in the light of our Christian faith, we may expect to see the face and to hear the voice of our Lord. We have followed the course of Biblical history down to the days of Christ; now is the time to retrace our steps to the origin of revelation. This is what Fr. de Lubac describes as follows:

> The New Testament writers, simultaneously and jointly, express the New Testament by the Old and spiritualize the Old by the New. As for us, who reflect on the New Testament as a constituted body of writing, we must, through historical exegesis, comment

this New Testament by means of the Old and then, conversely, comment the Old Testament by means of the New: a double operation, a double movement, a rhythm of which the alternate tenses cannot be distinguished except at the reflex period.[7]

We should have no doubt as to the objectivity and effectiveness of our vision of the face of Christ in the double mirror of the Old and New Testament for, in the words of Hugh of St. Victor (twelfth century), "all divine Scripture is one Book, and this unique Book is Christ, since all divine Scripture is fulfilled in him."[8]

St. Paul wrote to his disciple Timothy: "All Scripture is inspired of God and profitable for doctrine, for reproof, for correction, for instruction in righteousness" (2 Tim 3:16). Indeed! The aim is edification, in the sense of building up the faith. Still, we have some difficulty figuring out the benefit we can draw from a list of obscure chieftains in Edom (Gen 36:40), from ritual prescriptions for sanitizing spots of mildew on a house wall (Lev 14:33), or from the uninhibited realism of stories which would have been censured in the Victorian era, were it not that they are found in the Bible. Surely the profit, if any, which may be expected from reading such Old Testament sections, is rather doubtful. Would it be, then, that they are susceptible of another interpretation, in addition to the obvious meaning of the letter? And how is this other interpretation to be secured? The Fathers of the Church were fully aware of the problem. St. Augustine wrote:

> Whenever it is possible to understand not one sense, but two or more senses from the same words of Scripture, even if the meaning intended by the writer remains obscure, this creates no hazard, if we can show from other scriptural passages that each one of these senses is consonant with truth. The student of the sacred word, however, must apply himself to ascertaining the meaning intended by the author through whom the Holy Spirit has delivered this particular Scripture.[9]

These are brave words, too abstract to be effective; they leave us without a criterion to discern with certitude the sense "intended by the author."

The assumption of a sense, or senses, *other* than the

obvious meaning of the letter, is at the root of the allegorical method of interpretation. In fact this is exactly what the etymology of the word "allegory" suggests: ἀλληγορία, from ἄλλος and ἀγορεύω.[10] Mediaeval schoolmen in the West elaborated systematically a theory of the fourfold sense of the Scriptures: "The letter teaches what was done; the allegory what you must believe; the moral sense what you must do; the anagogy whereto you must tend."[11] The enumeration varies from one author to another, but the variants do not significantly alter the scheme as a whole.

In fact, the three derivative senses were often grouped together under the general rubric of "spiritual" sense, over against the "literal," or "historical," sense. The latter denomination relates to what mediaeval authors called *historia,* viz. the recitation of facts. There was a fairly general agreement that in the case of parables, like, for instance, the parable of the good Samaritan, the literal sense is not the story itself materially understood, but rather the point that is being made by the storyteller.[12] The theory of the four senses was used without restraint by the scholastics, and its artificiality provoked a demand for a more realistic attitude. Thus Thomas Aquinas, while upholding a legitimate recourse to the spiritual sense, insisted that "it is based on the literal sense and presupposes it."[13] The sixteenth-century Protestant scholars went further, denying the objective validity of the spiritual sense, under pretense of building their doctrine on the unshakable, but too narrow basis, offered by the letter of the sacred text.

Among the Eastern Fathers and writers, Theodoret of Kyros (ca. 393-460) had been generally successful in finding a middle road between pedestrian historicism and the acrobatics of allegorism:

> I ran into diverse commentaries and found that the commentators indulged in far-fetched allegories, while others did adapt the prophecy to some historical predicament, eager as they were to provide an interpretation meet for the Jews, rather than a food fit for babes in the faith. I thought it most advisable to flee from the former excess as much as from the latter.[14]

Allegory ought to be distinguished from one of its

subspecies, which plays a capital role in traditional hermeneutics and in the liturgical utilization of texts from the Old Testament. Whereas many allegories are derived from the letter of Scripture by way of rhetorical associations, some are firmly rooted in the very soil of history. They are not arbitrary figures, but objective types. The theological principle involved has been formulated very clearly by St. John Chrysostom (354-407). He distinguished those prophecies which consist of words, διὰ ῥημάτων, διὰ λόγου, from the prophecies consisting of things or deeds, διὰ πραγμάτων, διὰ τύπου:

> I will give you an example of prophecy by means of things, and of prophecy in words, regarding the same object: "He was led like a lamb to the slaughter and as a sheep before his shearer" (Is 53:7); that is a prophecy in words. But when Abraham took Isaac and saw a ram caught by his horns in a thicket, and actually offered the sacrifice (Gen 22:3-13), then he really proclaimed unto us, in a type, the salutary Passion.[15]

A similar distinction is used by Aquinas, in the article of the *Summa* quoted above (note 13): "God, who is the author of Holy Scripture, can use things and events to signify truth, as well as words. The former mode corresponds to the allegorical-typical sense of Scripture; the latter, to the literal sense."

This is concretely what happens: the Bible presents repeated instances of correlated historical events: the Exodus from Egypt and the new Exodus, viz. the return of the Babylonian exiles to their homeland; the miraculous crossing of the Red Sea, the fording of the Jordan by Joshua and the Israelites on their march into the promised land, and the baptism of Jesus in the Jordan, prototype of the sacrament of our regeneration and of our deliverance from sin and death. Thus do the Old Testament types prepare the revelation of the New, and the Gospel illumines the mysterious events of the past. Typology, therefore, appears to be an integral part of the divine economy, essentially linked with the progression of Sacred History toward its τέλος, its ultimate goal, the kingdom that is to come.

The first condition of validity for typological interpreta-

tion is that there be an ontological relationship between the
type and the typified mystery, by reason of the gradual realization, within time, of God's eternal design. Fr. de Lubac
remarks that the Church Fathers, when they compared the
sacrifice of Abraham with the sacrifice of Jesus Christ, may
have insisted overmuch on fortuitous details, but did not
err when they saw a link in depth between the two situations.[16]

If traditional hermeneutics is carried to its normal outcome, and typology must be involved in the process, it leads
to the discovery of what is described by some contemporary
Roman theologians as the *sensus plenior,* the "fuller sense,"
not superimposed upon Scripture from without, but drawn
from the potentiality of the letter by a process of homogeneous deduction. The neglect or rejection of the typological approach results unavoidably in spiritual impoverish-
ment, and it constitutes a serious fault of method. Some of
our colleagues in the teaching profession may be more
sensitive to the latter charge because it threatens their
academic respectability.

A final remark is in order at this point. Much of what
we wrote in the present chapter will not be accepted in
principle by independent critics not ready to recognize the
validity of the Judaeo-Christian revelation and the authority
of Tradition. But traditional hermeneutics is an "engaged"
discipline, not a mere academic exercize. For this reason,
some Christian scholars have felt impelled to distinguish
between the spiritual sense, as an inherent mode of the
scriptural text, and the spiritual understanding of Scripture,
as the personal gain of one who applies himself to the study
of the message; the latter is indispensable, for only "in thy
light shall we see light" (Ps 36:9), and only under the
intimate motion of the Spirit who first inspired Scripture,
can we expect to discern the face of our Christ shining amidst
the shadows of the past, as it has secretly shone for the
Forefathers.

The lengthy introduction which the above three chapters
represent was perhaps unnecessary; we hope nevertheless

that it may prove useful as a briefing, as we set out for the exploration we are going to undertake in the following chapters, searching the Old Testament for clues to the Christian mystery.

CHAPTER IV

In the Beginning

"In the beginning, God created heaven and earth." According to Hebrew tradition—emphatically *not* a live recording—the appearance of man on earth took place on the "sixth day" of creation, preceded by a period of preparation during which God sorted out the elements of this world[1] and disposed all things in orderly fashion, mustering them like his army (Gen 2:1).[2] The frame of sea and land, adorned with vegetation and teeming with living things, would be ready for Adam and Eve to dwell and multiply in it, managing the resources it offered according to the design of God. In this first creation account. Adam is not a personal name,[3] but a generic term, man, matching the categories of living creatures already mentioned: the fish (*dagah*), the birds (*'ôf*), and the cattle (*behêmah*), designated in Hebrew by collective nouns in the singular form. No concrete detail here about the creation of the woman; it is only said that God made the first two humans male and female, and that they would have dominion over the entire creation.

It is difficult to see in this narrative, or in the more

relaxed story that is told in the following chapters of Genesis, a realistic description of the origin of the human race. What we read is rather a series of statements about the Creator and his economy regarding mankind, as reflected in the traditions of the Hebrew people. We would be very ill-advised to equate the Biblical data with scientific hypotheses concerning the formation of the cosmos and the successive stages of its evolution. Tentative harmonizations are, to say the least, premature, and would result in artificial concordism: poor science, and poor exegesis.

There is a general agreement among sober-minded scholars with regard to the composition and age of the Biblical narratives on the creation.[4] The fact that they are given in the first three chapters of Genesis is no clue to their antiquity. Their attribution to Moses rests on the mere fact that the Book of Genesis was considered as the normal introduction to the description of the Mosaic institutions in their historical setup. In fact, the Book of Genesis, as we read it today, results from the compiling, probably during the post-exilic period, of local traditions, oral or partly written, originating in various districts of the Hebrew land, and conventionally distributed by the final redactor in a sort of genealogical framework, the "generations," *toldoth,* of heaven and earth (2:4), of Adam (5:1), of Noah (6:9), of the sons of Noah (10:1), of Shem (11:10), of Terah (11:27), of Ishmael (25:12), of Esau "who is Edom" (36:1), and of Jacob (37:2).

The opening narrative (Gen 1 to 2:4), attributed by the critics to a post-exilic theologian, is shaped as a logical, exhaustive classification of created things, which make their appearance on each day of the "first week," from the inanimate creatures, the celestial bodies, the ocean and the dry land, to the living things, fish and fowl, wild beasts and cattle, and up to man, who occupies a unique position between God and the world. It is interesting to compare the first creation story with Psalm 104, and it is not immaterial that the latter was appointed, in Byzantine usage, as the opening Psalm of Vespers, at the liturgical beginning of each new day. A footnote in the Jerusalem Bible remarks that Psalm 104 follows generally the order of the Genesis account. However, the laborious classifications of Genesis 1 stands in sharp contrast with the freer lyricism of the Psalm. Both may well have drawn from a common source.

It may be pure impressionism on my part. I visualize, when the Psalm is read in the church, the unique landscape of Mount Carmel, the lightning and thunder amidst the clouds running low along the range; the fragrant pine trees, the oleanders, the thickets of laurel, ilex and dwarf oaks, offering a shelter to birds and to wild game; the caves and clefts in the limestone cliffs, a refuge for the conies (v. 18); to the west, like the prow of a galley, the sharp profile of the "Sacred Cape," the *Rosh qadosh* of the Phoenician mariners, the jagged rocks battered by the waves of the sea; toward the rising sun, the villages and the golden fields of the fertile *'Emeq;* and above all, the memory of Elijah the wonderworker, champion of the true God over against the priests of Baal.

A thematic similarity between the Biblical narrative and some ancient Near Eastern cosmogonies cannot be denied. Much attention was given during the early decades of the twentieth century to the mythological texts from Mesopotamia, which were considered by some scholars, too hastily, as the sources of the Hebrew stories on creation. More recently, the religious epics discovered at Ras Shamra on the Syrian coast, in the language and the script of Ugarit,[5] have made us more fully acquainted with the religion of the Phoenicians, thus far known only through the secondhand reports of the Greek mythographers.

The Oriental cosmogonies describe the organization of our world by supernatural, personal beings, the gods; the creation of man out of material elements animated by a vital fluid; and man's station as intermediary between the gods and the animal world. Reduced to these generic elements, the theme of these cosmogonies can be compared with the Biblical theme of the origins.

The resemblance, however, stops here and soon gives way to essential differences: the major gods, who appear

from nowhere, having themselves been created, their messengers and satellites, are in a continuous struggle, as they
strive to bring order in an eternally preexisting chaos, and
vie against each other to gain control of the various depart-
ments of the universe and to lord it over men, their creatures,
whom they greatly need, for who would offer sacrifices?

> When the heaven above had not been named,
> the land below, its name had not been called;
> the primordial abyss, their begetter;
> the tumultuous Tiamat, mother of them all,
> their waters all mixed in one.
> No bulrush in the marshland, no reed to be seen.
> Of the gods, none had been caused to be;
> no name yet had been called, no destiny fixed;
> Then were the gods created.[6]

In short, a theogony, within the general framework of a
cosmogony, the stage being built for the apparition and
growth of primitive mankind. Topical features differentiate
slightly the Oriental and the Phoenician varieties; early
Mesopotamian civilization arose from the Chaldaean plains:
a landscape of sea, canals, marshes, the uncertain contours
of alluvial flats perpetually altered by the spring floods of
the twin rivers, Euphrates and Tigris, the tidal waves from
the Persian gulf, from which strange fish-gods brought arts
and techniques to the first inhabitants of the land, the
advancing delta.[7] Towns, temples, and cities were established
on higher ground, protected by dikes and levies, the building
material being the ubiquitous bricks of sun-dried clay, and
the first brick mould serving as a convenient divider between
the primaeval chaos and the humanization of the cosmos.[8]
The Phoenician landscape, by contrast, is clear-cut: the
mountain rising steep above a narrow coastal strip, and the
Tyrian seas swelling against the rocky shores of the Lebanese
coast, are the stage set for the conflict of the gods: Aleyn
Baal, the storm-god, who reigns on high and rides the clouds,
against the forces of the deep, to which he assigns inviolable
limits, and who restores life to a land cursed by Môt, his
arch-enemy, god of death and drought.[9]

The opposition between the Biblical doctrine and the
Eastern cosmogonies, no matter how much the latter may

differ among themselves, is radical. It has even been suggested that the scheme of Genesis 1 to 2:4 may have been intended as a polemic statement over against the pagan cosmogonies, an hypothesis not lacking scriptural support.[10] At any rate, the religion of the Old Testament cannot be understood otherwise than as a straight monotheism. The uniqueness of God is the first dogma of the Biblical faith. We need not be alarmed by the fact that God is referred to in the very first verse of Genesis as Elohim, a plural noun, which has been explained by the grammarians as a plural of majesty. In fact, Elohim is not a name, but rather a Semitic idiom for the supernatural beings, the gods, of whom El is the father. The God of the Old Testament is and will remain unnamed, because no human mind, no human word can possibly grasp nor express his essence. He reveals himself as transcendent, not merely first among other gods. He can have no equal, no rival. He is, in truth and super-eminently, κατ' ἀλήθειαν, κατ' ἐξοχήν, God.

He is Creator. Creation is a free act of the Eternal who is neither limited nor conditioned by the inertia or the resistance of matter. It means absolute beginning; "before" the creation, God is, nobody and nothing is; when mediaeval theologians speak of God creating the world from nought, *ex nihilo,* we are not to understand "nought" as a pseudo-being, out of which something would be produced. Something that was not, now is, by God's will and word. This we can understand somehow, for it involves no contradiction, but men need images drawn out of time and space in their attempt to give an account of that which is humanly unaccountable. To that effect, the authors of the Old Testament had to demythologize the cosmogonies of their pagan neighbors and to exorcize their polytheism and its pantheistic implications.

Traces of this cathartic process abound in Scripture. When we read that "the earth was without form and void," in Hebrew *tôhu wabôhu* (Gen 1:2),[11] this does not refer to the eternally preexisting chaos in which the pagan gods were allegedly created, but to the theoretical stage of the world as produced by God, prior to the distinction and

organization of its constitutive elements. It does not designate
an actual state of the material universe, which was never
without a form, even though that form defies imagination.
The Biblical authors did not, or cared not, eliminate all
mythological features, ingrained in the common literary
habits of Near Eastern poetry, but these were, so to speak,
deactivated. The abyss, *tehôm* in Hebrew, over which darkness reigned, is no longer identified with the "tumultuous
Tiamat" of the Babylonian epic,[12] but with the face of the
sea, set in perpetual motion by the Spirit of God (Gen 1:2).
The demythologization of the heavenly bodies created on
the fourth day is complete. Sun and moon, the highest cosmic
deities of the Babylonians, respectively Shamash and Sin,
have become "two great luminaries in the skies," dividing
the day from the night (Gen 1:14-18). As for the phases of
the moon, they are much appreciated by the Hebrews for
fixing their calendar of months, when the lunar crescent
appears in the sky, and the full moon shines over the Passover night. No trace remains of the detailed instructions
which Marduk, supreme god of Babylon, gives to the divine
NANNAR (Sin), who is ordered, first, to show two horns,
then the half of his circular crown, and then to turn himself
full-face.[13] On the fifth day of creation, God makes the huge
sea monsters, *tannînim gedôlim* (Gen 1:21), impressive
enough as zoological species (and also as mariners' yarns),
but destitute of the semi-divine personality of the linguisti-
cally related *Tnn* of the Ugaritic poems, or of *Ltn,* which
corresponds to the Hebrew Leviathan. The Tannîn and the
Leviathan have retained some of their mythological flavor
in such poetical texts as Isaiah 27:1, "Leviathan the elusive,
crooked serpent, Tannîn, the dragon of the sea," (cf. Ps 74:14
and Job 3:8). It is interesting to note, however, that Job,
in spite of his hyperboles, downgrades Leviathan to the
rank of a vulgar crocodile (41:1), just as he does Behemoth,
the hippopotamus (40:15).[14]

　　Creation, for the Old Testament writers, is not the battlefield of the gods, nor a meaningless turmoil of elements,
but a mirror in which we may see, under certain conditions,
a reflection of the face of God. It is therefore possible, on

the basis of Genesis, to formalize the doctrinal contents of the Hexaemeron as follows: All things were created by the power of the Word; God said, "Let there be...," "and it was so." The world was created in hierarchic order, each creature being assigned its rank and function. Through his Spirit, God is the author of life, so that the living species, each according to its seed, has in itself the principle and pattern of growth and perpetuation. Man was created last, with unique endowments, in the image and after the likeness of his Creator, unto the fulfilling of his destiny. Theological sidelines are implied, rather than expressed; the author of Genesis suggests indirectly, but clearly enough, that the scheme realized in the space of six days, followed by the Creator's rest on the seventh, is connected aetiologically with typical Hebrew institutions: the perpetual week, liberated from the phases of the moon for the reckoning of time, the sabbath and its derivatives.

Old Testament monotheism is not to be confused with philosophical monism, which would make the Biblical concept of creation untenable. Either it would "freeze" God in his own essence and make the universe part of his incommunicable being, or make God the supreme abstraction, presiding impassibly over the interactions of individual monads having each one in itself the principle and pattern of its existence and depending on none other for the furtherance of its aims. Instead, the Bible represents God active in the world which he has created, entering in lively conversation with Adam and Eve, Cain and Abel, with Moses and the prophets, and visibly intervening in world events toward the fulfilment of his goals. These, of course, are anthropomorphisms, viz. figurative modes of speaking of God in human terms. But how else could a human being express the fact of his entering into relation with his Creator?
    Late Judaism had sensed this particular problem and tentatively thought of the possibility of a contact between the transcendence of God and his creatures, being established by means of intermediaries derived from the divine essence: the *Shekhînah* (Presence), the *Kabhôd* (Glory), the *Shem*

(Name), the *Metatron* (Guidance),[15] or by means of attributes conceptually distinct from the Essence, and implying a relation with the creatures. There is a certain similarity between the teaching of the mediaeval rabbis on the attributes of God and the Islamic doctrine of the Beautiful Names of Allah.[16]

Exceptionally, a few Muslim thinkers, consciously or unconsciously influenced by Christian thought, have been searching the Quran for possible analogies to the dogma of the Trinity: Allah; Jesus, whom Muhammad acknowledged as preeminent among God's envoys; and a holy Spirit, lifegiver and messenger of God's revealed truth.[17] There is, as a matter of fact, no solution to the problem of communication between the absolutely transcendent and the world of men, except if we conceive God as the Trinity of Persons, in accordance with the unanimous Tradition.

Unless there is found in the Old Testament a valid foundation for the dogma of the Trinity, we would have to acknowledge that there is a theological break between the Old and the New Testament. Such, however, is not the case. The Hebrews could rightly boast that there is no nation whose god "makes himself so near to them as the Lord our God does to us, whenever we call upon him" (Deut 4:7). However they could not penetrate the secret of God's life. The scriptural passages in which the nature of God's exclusive mystery is implied—not expressed—were due to remain for them riddles, or limited to inadequate analogies, for only in the light of the full revelation of the Gospel can these passages be truly understood; it is as if they had been written expressly for us, who come after the incarnation of the Son of God.

This should sober us, not make us arrogant. Nor does it mean two grades of revelation, but that God discloses himself according to what amount of truth men can profitably receive, in the concrete circumstances of their cultural development. In fact, the Hebrews were continually threatened in their monotheistic faith by the polytheism of their neighbors. There are secrets they could not bear yet, and there are secrets which even Christ, according to his humanity

—we are thinking here of the date of the Parousia—was not given to share. St. Athanasius, referring to this economy of delayed revelation, remarked that some logia were not pronounced "when the Logos, who was with God, put all things together, nor at any time prior to his being made a man, but only after the Word was made flesh."[18]

Extant in the Book of Genesis are a number of verses which have exercized the sagacity of the exegetes, and which early Christian commentators have interpreted as implicit testimonies to the trinitarian nature of the divine being. They tell of God creating the Universe and drafting a policy toward his human creatures, just as men would do when they are about to attend to a matter of importance, consider the *pro* and *con*, and decide on a course of action. Note the plurals and the forms of the verbs: "Let *us* make man in *our* image, after *our* likeness" (Gen 1:26); "Man is become as one of *us*, to know good and evil" (Gen 3:22); "Let *us* go down and there confound their language" (Gen 11:7).[19] There is here something more than plurals of majesty. Did God take counsel of his angels, an interpretation suggested by the Greek of Isaiah 9:5, where one of the Messiah's titles is "Angel of the Great Council"? Grammarians consider the formula "Let us" as a cohortative, a technical label which in fact covers a whole philosophy of language: I (subject) bring myself (object) to take such or such decision, and to pass to immediate action, as if the final resolution were taken jointly by several responsible persons. It would be imprudent, of course, to draw a full-fledged theology from these verses. It remains, however, that the Church Fathers, who exploited the theme, did not indulge in a worthless allegorism, but discerned, under these anthropomorphisms, a clue, however faint, of the societal nature of God.

Less striking at first glance, but perhaps more solid, is the fact, already noted in this chapter, that God is said to have created the world by the power of his Word and Spirit, not by separate instruments, not by commissioned agents, not by a Demiurge, not by intermediaries. God's Spirit was "soaring" (*merahéfeth*) upon the face of the deep (Gen

1:1), as the universal principle of life. God said the Word, and the world was made (Ps 33:6). Conversely, the world, because it was so created, bears witness to the life of God in the Trinity of Persons.

It all means, then, that the Word, the Logos, who would, in the fulness of time, become man, was present and active "in the beginning." The Gospel of St. John becomes the indispensable key to the understanding of the first chapter of Genesis: "In the beginning was the Word, and the Word was with God, and the Word was God. All things were made by him, and without him was not any thing that was made.... And the Word was made flesh, and dwelt among us" (John 1:1, 3, 14). It is, of a truth, the face of our Christ which is mirrored in the story of the creation, when God broke the silence of eternity,[20] and when the vision of God's eternal Wisdom became reality.[21] The creative Word is the same as the Incarnate Word, and when Zacharias prophetically hailed Christ as the Rising Sun from on high, we were given to understand that he would run the race for us: as a man goes forth to do his daily work (Ps 104:23), so will the Son of God, sallying forth from his chamber (Ps 19:5), shine upon all who sit in darkness and in the shadow of death.

CHAPTER V

The Protevangel

On the "sixth day" of creation, God said: "Let us make man in our image, after our likeness" (Gen 1:26). Shall we make a formal distinction between "image" (εἰκών) and "likeness" (ὁμοίωσις)? And why is it that the Hebrew uses two different particles: *be*, "in," and *ke*, "after," "according to"? It seems that a theological theory developed on the sole basis of such distinctions would be open to a serious charge of artificiality. One thing is certain: the redundant formula, easily explained by the fondness of Hebrew writers for parallelism, means at least that man is related to his Creator by a unique kinship which sets him apart from all other creatures and points to his destiny.[1]

What this destiny will be, we learn from the second story on the creation and fall of Adam, and of the first announcement of salvation, the so-called Protevangel (Gen ch. 2 and 3). Here, the general organization of the cosmos is taken for granted. A brief summary is given by way of introduction, or rather as a transition between the elaborate scheme of chapter one and the story of Adam and Eve, according to a popular tradition possibly committed to writing some time before the exile. It abounds in picturesque features, as the narrator muses among seemingly irrelevant details.[2] But let this not deceive us; our storyteller makes his point at least as well as the systematic writer of the Hexaemeron.

The action takes place in the "garden in Eden" (Gen 2:8).[3] It is described as a well-watered orchard in the midst of an otherwise arid steppe, somewhere in Mesopotamia, as we may surmise from the mention of the Tigris and the Euphrates, two of the four rivers of "paradise" (Gen 2:14). Imagine a criss-cross of irrigation ditches, the greenery of shade and fruit trees, carefully tended beds of vegetables, emerald patches of late cereals, long after a meager harvest has been gathered from the sun-parched fields round about. Whatever water is left disappears in the sand, where a few reeds absorb the last traces of moisture.

Dramatis personae: God, known from now on as Yahweh, usually rendered in English by "the Lord," or, in composition with Elohim, "the Lord God." He is the master of the garden, in which he loves to stroll in the cool of the evening (Gen 3:8).

Adam, fashioned out of red clay, the *adamah*—hence his surname—and made into a living creature through God breathing the breath of life into his nostrils (Gen 2:7). Adam will never lose his connection with the earth from which he came and to which he shall return (Gen 3:19). He is appointed responsible caretaker of the garden (Gen 2:15). The entire district is teeming with all sorts of animals; God brings them to Adam, who unerringly identifies them by name (Gen 2:19-20). Obviously, Adam is perfectly attuned to the order of creation, which God has pronounced good, even very good (Gen 1:31). No realistic painting here, nor abstract theologizing. The entire setting reminds one of a Douanier Rousseau painting.

Eve, Adam's wife. God made her out of a rib of Adam, upon whom he had caused a deep sleep to fall.[4] Thus she is designated as *ishah*, a wo-man, from *ish*, man (Gen 2:21-24). She will be called later Eve, *Hawwah*, because she will become the mother of all living (root *h-y/w-h*) (Gen 3:20).

The serpent, a strange beast, creeping out of nowhere,

unpredictable, repulsive to humans, trying to be persuasive, and described here as unusually crafty (Gen 3:1).

We find in the first three chapters of Genesis the rationale of man's destiny. It is suggested, in the colorful narratives on creation, that man, in the person of Adam, the father of the race,[5] had been endowed with everything he needed to enter the role assigned to him by the Creator, and to grow, physically and spiritually, so that God's own features would become recognizable in his human icon. Here is how St. Irenaeus, commenting the text of Genesis, expresses this:

> It behoved man, after he was born, to grow: growing, he would come of age; being of age, he would multiply; having multiplied, he would grow strong; being strong, he would be glorified; glorified, he would see his master, for God himself shall be seen of man; now the vision confers incorruption, and incorruption brings one close to God.[6]

Irenaeus' climactic reasoning follows the chronological order, which is particularly germane to our thinking: thus do we refer to Christ, following St. Paul, as the "second Adam," who came to consummate the work undertaken at creation. This is the final objective in the light of which we are called to honor the very charter of our existence as creatures, since "Christ, the Logos of God, our Lord, out of overflowing love, has made us what we are, that he may dispose us to be that which he is."[7] In this consists our salvation, which must be understood primarily as deification ($\vartheta\acute{\epsilon}\omega\sigma\iota\varsigma$), a participation in the very life of God,[8] in the measure of our receptivity and of our response.

There seems to have been some confusion in the "stage directions" for the drama of the temptation and of the fall of man: two trees are mentioned in the description of the garden in Eden: "the tree of life in the midst of the garden, and the tree of the knowledge of good and evil" (Gen 2:9). Adam is allowed to pick fruits from every tree, except one. But which is the forbidden tree? Would it be the tree of life? In the temptation scene, Eve seems to think so: there it stands in front of her, in the midst of the garden, where

God has planted it (Gen 3:3). Life belongs to God, and God is understandably jealous of his prerogative. After the sin has been committed, he will ironize: "Does that man think he is going to live forever?" (Gen 3:22). Or is the forbidden fruit growing on the tree of the knowledge of good and evil. As a matter of fact, God had said to Adam: "Thou shalt not eat of it, for in the day that thou eatest thereof, thou shalt surely die" (Gen 2:17).[9] The difficulty seems to result from the fusion of two different traditions, as the conflate reading of verse 22 might indicate. Taken as a whole, however, textual evidence points rather to the tree *of the knowledge of good and evil* as the forbidden tree. Note the underlined words; the tree is not called simply tree of good and evil, for obviously the same tree does not yield two kinds of fruit, some good, some bad. Evil has no place in Eden, no more than in the kingdom that is to come. There can be no experiential knowledge of evil except after sin; prior to the fall, evil can only be conceived as a "possible," contingent upon a morally wrong choice. Adam and Eve in the garden are, in all the senses of the word, two "innocents."

The action, chapter 3, takes the form of a psychological drama. Eve, beguiled by the serpent, induces Adam in eating from the forbidden fruit; Adam blames the whole thing on his wife, and Eve on the serpent. Having heard their statements, God pronounces his verdict in the reverse order: first on the serpent, then on the woman, and last on Adam, who is held accountable for his wife and for those who shall be born from their union (Gen 3:14-21).

The tempter is definitely to be identified with the Evil Spirit in the guise of the serpent. His mysterious personality manifests itself from time to time in the course of the Old Testament under a variety of aliases; Satan, the latest of his avatars, figures only in post-exilic writings, and this rarely. The pre-exilic writings refer to invisible beings whose hostile, vexatious character God eventually uses for the punishment of evildoers. Oriental influences tend to make the Evil Spirit the Adversary par excellence, the Accuser, the Calumniator, ὁ διάϐολος, "he who takes a bite" (Syriac *okhel qarçô*). His impotent strife against God shall continue to the last day. The Bible, however, shows no trace of the absolute dualism of Iranian thought, with its two coeternal principles whose irreducible opposition rules the events of this world. It is clear that the temptation which befalls Eve is of Satanic origin. The fall of the first human couple is not presented by the author of Genesis as a natural failure due to ignorance, weakness or common malice, but to downright rebellion: never mind what God ordered or forbade; there is the fruit; they desire it, they bite into it, and that is that!

Some day, Christ, the second Adam, would also be tempted by the devil, after the forty days of his fast (Mt 4:1-11). The strategy of the tempter is consistently clear: in the garden, he cavils on the instructions which Yahweh gave to Adam, and confuses Eve, who does not wish for anything more than to be persuaded, allured as she is by the appearance of the fruit. On the Mount of Temptation, the devil argues from God's words in the Scriptures—the weapons have been updated—rather imprudently, for Jesus, the Logos, counters with other words from Scripture, *his own words,* and cuts short the discussion with a curt dismissal.

God would not have his servants exempt from temptation. Mary, the second Eve, was troubled at the words of the Angel of the Annunciation, but did not allow her anxiety to grow into positive doubt and, after a fleeting moment of indecision, pronounced the irrevocable *fiat:* "Be it unto me according to thy word" (Lk 1:29, 38).[10] St. Joseph also experienced what amounted for him to a temptation, when he was thinking of repudiating his bride, and it took the visitation of an angel to make him overcome his doubt (Mt 1:18-21).[11]

The immediate consequence of the sin of Adam and Eve is the statutory penalty of death, to be visited on them and on their descendants for their own sins, for "the wages of sin is death" (Rom 6:23). Conversely, death, through the apprehension and anxiety it causes in us, is frequently a cause of doubt, despair and sin. Christ, because he is the second Adam, and because he was born to fulfill man's destiny, which cannot be thwarted or forfeited, submitted himself to death; Mary, his mother, was not excepted; but death, through the death and resurrection of Christ, has lost its sting (1 Cor 15:55).

Death is not the only consequence. Sin, Adam's sin and our sins have thrown disorder into creation, incoherence, contradiction, hostility. St. Augustine, referring to the world of his sinful youth, calls it *regio dissimilitudinis,* a land where everything is topsy-turvy, nothing makes sense, nothing is constructive. It looks as if we are witnessing a renewed outbreak of the forces of chaos; after our hymns to progress, we suddenly realize the absurdity of our spiritual, economic, and ecological predicament.

In all that gloom, a voice is heard; it was heard even before the Word of God came upon the prophets and before he was made man. In the very act of sentencing the culprits, the Judge made it known that the Evil One would be curbed and ultimately defeated, even by those whom he had deceived. "I will put enmity between thy seed and *her* seed; *it* shall bruise thy head, and thou shalt bruise *his* heel" (Gen 3:15, King James version). Instead of *it* for the Hebrew *hû,* indetermined as to gender, the Revised Standard Version has the masculine *him,* following the Greek αὐτός, viz. "a descendant of the woman"; the precision of the Greek, anterior to the adoption of the LXX by the Christian Church, is the basis of the messianic interpretation of the Fathers, in the strict sense. According to the Latin Vulgate, it is the woman herself, *ipsa,* who shall crush the head of the serpent, and the western Church as a whole has understood that Mary would avenge Eve. St. Irenaeus, commenting on Eve being an Old Testament type of the Theotokos, explains how there has been, so to speak, a "turning about" from Mary to Eve, *recirculationem, recircumlationem,* seeing that "there is no other way to untie the knots (of sin) than by reversing what was done in tying them."[1] The reading of the Vulgate was used by a number of Roman theologians intent upon developing a Marian theology methodologically autonomous, rather than as a part of the doctrine on Christ.

Genesis 3:15 forms what has been called appropriately

the "Protevangel," namely the glad tidings of God pursuing the plan he had eternally conceived and which he would bring to conclusion, no matter what the cost. The Protevangel is definitely not the announce in court of an eventual paroling, contingent upon good behavior, of repentent sinners. It is rather a prophecy, soon to be followed in the Book of Genesis by the symbols of a future deliverance: the dove which Noah let out of the ark (Gen 8:9-12), and the rainbow (Gen 9:13).[13] In fact, the Protevangel is the first genuine prophecy of the incarnation of the eternal Son of God, and the unconditional proclamation of his future victory over Satan. The prophecy is long-range; later prophets would be kept in suspense regarding the time of the Second Coming, and the secret hour of the consummation would be revealed to no one, not even to the Son (Mt 24:36, only in the Greek).

Nothing in the Protevangel is said about death, the penalty of sin, still hanging over us. Yet we hear an accent of elation, the sound of a wild paean at the prospect of the monster's defeat, in spite of its frantic efforts to get at the woman's heel.[14] She will tramp him under foot and crush his ugly head, like the son of Mary trampling down death by death, as we sing in triumph, θανάτῳ θάνατον πατήσας, *smertiyu smert popravij.*

The fourth chapter of Genesis is marked by a slight change in the mode of narration. The authors of the first three chapters pictured the creation of the world, the appearance and the fall of man as they could imagine it. We would not dare to label this as myth, lest we be misunderstood, since "myth" has become, mistakenly, synonymous with pure fiction, a tale without reality. We afe dealing here with a literary form, no matter what we call it, the function of which is to give coherent expression to truths and events of a religious nature which cannot possibly be enunciated or described in empirical terms. A radical demythologization— *Entmythologisierung*—a term coined by German theologians, with a view of reaching the objective contents expressed by this medium, is neither desirable nor possible, for there is an organic connection between contents and form; the latter cannot be neglected or regarded as of little account without the doctrinal substance being compromised. But it should always be possible to determine what is meant, if we consider positively the figurative details which are the vehicles of truth. We believe that the formulae used by the sacred writers working under the charism of inspiration ought to be interpreted in this way.

The style of the fourth chapter of Genesis is a variety of the literary form of the creation stories; it is properly *Urgeschichte*, history of origins. Human inventions, institutions, techniques, are traced back to eponym heroes of whom nothing is remembered, but through whom we are informed of the presumed origin of realities which in many instances are still with us. Among the ancients, the context was invariably mythological: thus arts and techniques had been taught to the Babylonians by the messengers of Ea, who emerged successively from the Persian Gulf. In Egypt, Thot and his satellites had instructed the scribes and the builders of temples.

The Biblical account shows nothing of this mythology. We are presented in chapter 4 with a catalogue of all the firsts which occurred in the early generations of men: Cain, the first "tiller of the ground" and Abel, the first "keeper of sheep" (Gen 4:2-3); Enoch, the first to "build a city," a man who "walked with God, and he was not, for God took him" (Gen 5:24); Jabal, the first nomadic herdsman, "father of such as dwell in tents" (Gen 4:20); his brother Jubal, the first musician (Gen 4:21); Tubal Cain "an instructor of every artificer in brass and iron" (Gen 4:22). Not only achievements but failures also are recorded: thus Cain is the first murderer, and there are a few characters whom we have some difficulty to appraise: Lamech, the first bigamist, a bully bent upon vengeance; now is this the natural violence of a fierce temperament, or the birth of an institution designed to force arbitration on feuding clans? (Gen 4:19, 23).

As a matter of fact, the two series do not run parallel: good men, and bad men; good and bad are mixed, until the day when the wheat and the tares shall be separated. But

God is at work, invisibly, silently. His Word and Spirit are active in everything that is constructive, over against the recurring forces of destruction. The early Christian apologists, little inclined to find some good outside Christianity, credited the Logos with whatever they approved of among the pagans.[15] St. Justin: "What the philosophers and law-givers uttered or perceived correctly, this they did by perceiving and contemplating something of the Logos. . . . Christ was in part known of Socrates, for Christ is the Logos who was and is in all things."[16] And Clement of Alexandria said of the philosophers that they were "dreaming the Truth," ὀνειρώττουσαν τὴν ἀλήθειαν.[17]

The description of the early generations of men according to Genesis 4, which we call a history of origins, ought not to be placed on par with Prehistory, Anthropology, or what French scholars call Human Palaeontology. What is common to these disciplines and with the first eleven chapters of Genesis is merely that they deal with the predicament of early man. However they consider their common object from entirely different points of view. The scientist uses the concept of evolution as a working hypothesis, and tentatively describes what the successive stages of that evolution were, by analyzing and interpreting the prehistoric remains which are his material. He traces back what presumably is the biological ancestry of modern man, with a view to delimiting as narrowly as possible the margin of passage from sub-human primates to *homo*.

Biblical scholars and theologians are not directly concerned with these preliminaries to mankind. They take over where scientific procedure leaves off, and, short of blind prejudice, they should have no quarrel with the scientist, nor the scientist with them. Their material is provided by the scriptural record. They consider man as actually in possession of all his natural endowments, fully accountable for his acts and master of his fate; environmental factors, cultural progress or regress, important though they be, remain incidental. A clue to this may perhaps be the fact that the Bible represents Adam and Eve, in the very instant of their creation, as responsible adults; the human species, in the ancestry which evolutionary theories attribute to it, had not come of age yet, and, as such, is out of the normal range of theology.

Even if theology is kept within its proper bounds, it should not overdraw the distinction between the successive covenants of God with mankind which are reported in the Bible; they are rather modalities of a single economy. To be sure, the covenant with Abraham seems to reduce to the proportions of an ethnic privilege the covenant with Noah, which was open to all mankind; but is it not written that "in Abraham's seed shall all the nations of the earth be blessed" (Gen 22:18)? And what is new in the New Testament is not the covenant itself, but that the covenant was sealed in the blood of Christ; therefore the eucharistic anaphora of the Latin Church calls it "the new, and eternal covenant."

Nor should the orders of creation and of redemption be so sharply distinguished as to suggest that, due to the failure of the former, a radically new plan had been forced upon God in order to rescue what could be salvaged of his work.[18] God's eternal decision to associate man to his own blessedness is irrevocable, and the incarnation of his son is seen as a means of promoting this unique objective. Nevertheless the question has been raised whether, if it were not for sin, the Word of God would have become incarnate? I must confess here that I am little inclined to hypothetical speculations of the type: "What would have happened if . . . the situation had been radically different from what it actually was." Surely this is a shortcoming on my part. While the redemption from the penalties due to sin, a ransom, the satisfaction of a debt toward God, what is called "atonement" in the narrow sense, are indeed essential factors in the theology of the Incarnation and the doctrine on the work of Christ, it remains that the Eastern Fathers of the Church generally considered that the deification of man (θέωσις), whether he had sinned or not, justified abundantly that the Logos would be made man. On this we may rest the case.

CHAPTER VI

The Promise to the Fathers

There are two periods in the development of the Old Testament revelation which, observed from our own station in history, appear especially oriented toward the future: the period of the Patriarchs, precariously living as semi-nomads in the midst of the Canaanite landed peasantry and sustained by the God-inspired dream which had called them out of the land of their origins; and the post-exilic period, when the returning exiles sought vainly an escape from the never-ending problems of the reconstruction. In either case, the Biblical narratives exhibit a thrust forward in time or even beyond time, which somehow contrasts with the account of the day by day struggling of Moses for the establishment of his new nation, or with the illusory stability of the Hebrew kingdoms.

The Book of Genesis describes the age of the Hebrew Patriarchs as the continuous expansion of a privileged group of men, party to a covenant originated by God, and which would receive its charter as a nation in the days of Moses. This process of expansion is correlative, at each generation, with a process of elimination of marginal or undesirable elements, which might have vitiated the entire scheme.

From the very first moment, the terms of the covenant with Abraham provide that its benefits should one day be extended to all mankind; not that the original pact would be denounced or that modifying clauses would be added to it, but rather that its essential dispositions would be transposed from the historical to the transcendent level. Our purpose in the present chapter will be to summarize as concretely as possible, through selections from the narratives of Genesis, God's way with the Patriarchs, without losing from sight the final objective of their journey.

The promise, several times renewed in the course of Patriarchal history, is not unilateral. It is rather a solemn pact between Yahweh and the Abrahamides, which is described with a luxury of detail in Genesis 15:7-21. God said to Abraham:

> Bring me a heifer three years old, a she goat three years old, a ram three years old, a turtle dove and a pigeon. And he brought him all these, but he did not cut the birds in two. . . . As the sun was setting, a torpor fell on Abram and lo, a fright of great darkness fell upon him. . . . When the sun had gone down and it was dark, behold, a smoking firepot and a flaming torch passed between these pieces. On that day, Yahweh had made a covenant with Abram, saying: To thy descendents I give this land from the river of Egypt to the Great River, the Euphrates.

The scene thus described is a Semitic ritual of alliance, a *berith*. A sacrifice is offered, and the victims are disposed in rows, the larger ones having been previously split in halves, somewhat like the parcels of the prosphorae are arranged on the *diskos* at the table of preparation. The contracting parties walk ritually between the victims, pledging their readiness to be similarly quartered, if either would fail to observe his terms in the covenant. In the Genesis story, the parties to the covenant are God and Abraham, who is promised a countless descendence and possession of the land under condition of trust and obedience. God appears under the symbols of a divine fire, a smoking firepot and a lighted torch, to which little attention has been paid by my fellow exegetes. This imagery points to a Mesopotamian origin—likely in the case of Abraham, the emigrant from Ur Kasdim—the same ideographic character serving to designate, with only slight modifications, the god of fire, fire, a portable oven or firepot (*kinûnu, tinûru*), or a torch (*dipârum*).[1]

The journey of the Hebrew Patriarchs had begun in the belt of pastures surrounding the irrigated gardens of Ur Kasdim in Lower Mesopotamia, where semi-nomadic tribes grazed their sheep and brought them to the city market. These shepherds were issued from Shem, son of Noah. Yahweh appeared to Abram son of Terah, and ordered him out of the fields of Ur: "Go from thy country, thy kindred and thy father's house, to the land I will show thee. I shall make thee into a great nation and bless thee, and through thee shall all the families on earth be blessed" (Gen 12:1-3). This meant breaking away from the ancestral past. Already Shem, the eponym of the race, had been separated by God himself from his brothers Ham and Japhet, relegated respectively to Africa and non-descript regions of northern Eurasia (Gen 10:1). The process of selection had begun. In obedience to God's order, Abraham and his family took to the road, frequented by migrating herdsmen, round about the arid steppe of what the Syrians today call the Djezireh.[2] Further texts of Genesis, as well as archaeological evidence, suggest a steady acquaintance with the Aramaeans of Paddan-Aram, a district relatively abundant in water: the green belt and the wells of Urfa, the sources of the Balikh, the springs of Arab Punar. They crossed the Euphrates, and we can follow their traces through settled Aramaean districts: Neirab, the "entrance gate," Aleppo, Hama, Damascus, the table-land of Bashan, the notorious Djôlan Heights. They forded the Jordan into what was still for them a land of promise. This first water crossing—the "bridge of Jacob's daughters" in modern Arabic lore—is to be the first link in a long chain of types: the miraculous crossing of the Red Sea by the Israelites whom Moses would lead out of Egypt; the fording of the Jordan toward Jericho after forty years in the wilderness, and the first act of the conquest and occupation of Canaan; the baptism of Christ in the Jordan, hallowing the waters of the historic river, as the sign and authenticating seal of our regeneration.

Having crossed into Canaan, the Hebrew Patriarchs remained in contact with their Aramaean cousins. Matrimonial
ties and treaties of friendship formed between them a permanent, even though loose, bond. The dialect of Canaan
would from now on become the language of the Hebrews.
The name of Abram, "Exalted is the (divine) Father," became Abraham (Gen 17:5).[3] His wife Saraï, "the Queen,"
became Sarah (Gen 17:15). Two generations later, Jacob
concluded with his Aramaean in-laws, after lengthy discussions, bordering at times on the ludicrous, an agreement for
the delimitation of grazing rights in Transjordan. The pile of
stones which they erected as a monument, *yegar shahadûthâ,*
"the mound of the witness," would be translated into
Hebrew, word for word, *Gal'êd,* Gilead (Gen 31:47). No
repudiation or elimination here, but a sharp distinction, which
nothing would obliterate.

Each station on the road of the Patriarchs on the soil of
Canaan is lightened by an apparition of God, a further step
in the revelational process, and a corresponding elimination
of "dropouts." Abraham stops at Shechem, where he builds
an altar to Yahweh, who had manifested himself at the oak
of Moreh, "the Preceptor" (Gen 12:6). Jacob, revisiting the
site on his return from Aram, purchases there a piece of land
(Gen 34:19), and buries under the sacred oak the domestic
idols which his wife Rachel had stowed away (Gen 35:4;
cf. 31:19, 34): a clean sweep of all the pagan past. . . . One
day Jesus, thirsty and weary from a long march, would sit
down beside the well which Jacob had dug, and announce his
Evangel to a Samaritan woman who came to draw water
(John 4:5ff; cf. Gen 33:19-20).[4]

Proceeding southward, Abraham had pitched his tent between Bethel and Ai (Gen 12:8; 13:3). There, a new separation took place.[5] It was decided by mutual agreement that
Abraham's nephew, Lot, who had emigrated with him from
Ur Kasdim, would from then on pasture his flocks in the
southern part of the Jordan rift and in the 'Arabah described—euphemistically—as a garden of Yahweh (Gen
13:8-12). Lot became the incestuous father of Moab and
Ammon, definitely eliminated from the line of succession

(Gen 19:30-38). After the birth of Isaac, the long-expected heir born of Sarah in her old age, Ishmael, the son whom Hagar, the Egyptian bondwoman, had borne to Abraham, was exiled in the desert, where he lived as a free bowman, a proud nomad, "a wild ass of a man, his hand against all, the hands of all against him" (Gen 16:12 and 21:20-21). Ishmael would be present at the side of Isaac at the funeral of their father (Gen 25:9) as, one generation later, Esau and Jacob would bury Isaac (Gen 35:29). Radically eliminated are the south Arabian chieftains and the Midianites, issued of Qeturah, whom Abraham had taken for wife after the death of Sarah (Gen 25:1-4). As for the descendents of the concubines, they are lost from sight, somewhere to the East, under the common appellation of *Benê Qédem,* some of whom would sporadically emerge in later Hebrew literature as paragons of wisdom, challenging even the sages of Israel (Gen 25:6). Of Isaac's two sons, Esau, father of the Edomites (Gen 36:9)—a half-witted, hairy, uncouth wild hunter, who married "out of meeting" Hittite girls who became a "bitterness of spirit" to their mother-in-law Rebekah (Gen 26:35), a contempter of his own birthright, cheated time and again by his brother Jacob (Gen 25:29ff and chapter 27)—is the last to be ousted from the family inheritance.

This leaves Jacob and his twelve sons, eponyms of the twelve tribes, the exclusive heirs of the promise made to Abraham. They would be gathered into one nation under the name of honor which Yahweh had given to the last of the Patriarchs, Israel, "He who wrestles with God" (Gen 32:28).

The line of election from Abraham to the twelve eponyms of the Hebrew tribes continued under historically conditioned modalities throughout the age of the monarchies, dominated as they were by a messianic conception which the prophets, who had promoted it, worked to purify and gradually to free from earthly ties, in view of the time when an authentic son of David would appear and inaugurate on earth a kingdom not of this earth.

If we eliminate the casualties left along the road

of the Patriarchs, we follow an uninterrupted chain of historical figures stretching through the entire Bible to Jesus Christ in his redemptive incarnation. These are listed, without commentaries, in the genealogies which St. Matthew and St. Luke placed at the beginning of their respective Gospels. Matthew proceeds in descending order, from Abraham to Jesus, born of Mary (Mt 1:1-16). Luke, in reverse order, starts from Jesus who, "being about thirty years of age, was believed to be the son of Joseph . . . son of Adam, who was God's" (Lk 3:23-28). The exegesis of the two genealogies is bristling with difficulties relative to their respective objects, methods, and to their discrepancies. The solution of these problems is not essential to the purpose of this essay. Some verses in the genealogy according to St. Matthew are of special interest, inasmuch as they show Christ thoroughly involved in the human predicament, no matter how inglorious. Thus, he happens to be a descendent of Juda by Tamar, who forced Juda, by a rather unorthodox stratagem, to fulfill his own obligations under the law of the levirate (Mt 1:3 and Gen 38:6-26). Christ descends from Boaz by Ruth the Moabitess, a foreigner (Mt 1:5); from Solomon, by "the one who had been Uriah's wife," ἐκ τῆς τοῦ Οὐρίου, *ex ea quae fuit Uriae* (Mt 1:6, cf. 2 Sam chapters 11 and 12); from Uzziah (Azariah), the leper king, a type of the suffering servant of Yahweh and of the Crucified, disfigured, withdrawn from human society, an object of repulsion, abandoned by friends and kin (Mt 1:8, cf. 2 Ki 15:5 and 2 Chr 26:19-21).

Our liturgies have drawn abundantly from the Biblical motif of divine election, which points persistently to the actual appearance of the Messiah, realizing on the historical level the expectation of all ages. It suffices to recall here the assignment of the two Sundays preceding the Nativity to the commemoration of the Forefathers and of the Ancestors of Our Lord, and, in the western usage, the solemn chanting by the deacon of the genealogy according to St. Matthew for the third nocturn of the Nativity and according to St. Luke for the Matins of the Epiphany.

The gallery of portraits admiringly and laboriously painted by the Siracide witnesses to the constant Jewish tradition of a succession of men and women who had been God's instruments for the fulfilment of his plan of redemption (Eccli ch. 44 to 50:21). The Epistle to the Hebrews takes up the theme and develops it in connection with the notion of faith as a saving power, stated unambiguously by the author of Genesis 15:6. "Abram believed in God's promise, and it was counted to him as justice."

The section of Genesis in which the geste of the Patriarchs is recorded is among the richest of the entire Bible in Christological applications through typology and allegorical interpretations. We shall select two outstanding examples, both for their intrinsic value as objective types and for their suggestive power as illustrations of the mystery fulfilled in Christ. The first is the episode of the sacrifice of Isaac (Gen 22:1-14), a favorite theme of the Fathers in their commentaries and homilies. Abraham is ordered by God to offer in sacrifice, on a hilltop in Canaan, his heir, still a boy, born of Sarah in her old age, through whom the promise of the covenant should receive a beginning of realization. Stunned by the enormity of the demand, the father resigns himself; he saddles the ass, splits the wood for the holocaust; Isaac himself shall carry the logs. This gruesome detail much impressed the Church Fathers, who saw in it a figure of Christ carrying his cross up to Calvary. To Isaac's question, "Where is the lamb for the sacrifice?" Abraham answers evasively: "Yahweh shall provide" *yir'êh Yahweh*. The narrator finds there an etymology of the name of the hill, which from then on shall be called Mount Môriyyah, hypothetically derived from the root *r-'-h*.[6] Now, an altar is built, the wood disposed for the sacrifice, the fire lighted, and as Abraham takes the knife to slay his son, the "Angel of Yahweh" stays his hand; a substitute victim is found: a ram caught by his horns in a thicket.

Literary criticism has interpreted the drama as an aetiological legend[7] destined to explain a later prescription of the Mosaic law, whereby every man is under obligation to put to death the first-born fruit of a domestic animal, in recognition of life being the exclusive property of Yahweh, whereas the first child born to a man must be redeemed by means of a substitutionary sacrifice (Ex 13:11ff, 34:19ff, Num 18:15ff). The hypothesis is solid. It should be remembered at this point that one day, in fulfilment of the legal precept, Jesus himself would be presented to the Temple by Joseph and Mary forty days after his birth, and his messianic identity would be acknowledged and proclaimed by Simeon and Ann the prophetess (Lk 2:22ff). The Church commemorates this event by the "Feast of the Meeting," the Ὑπαπαντή. It is known in the West as the "Purification of the Blessed Virgin" or, according to popular tradition, the Candlemas or *Chandeleur,* in reference to the offering of wax candles for the altar during the celebration of the Mass: "A light to lighten the Gentiles, and the glory of thy people Israel." The typological objective of the Genesis story, once cleared from the unessentials, is that we, the sinners on whose behalf Christ gave himself in unconditional obedience, shall be saved, as Isaac was saved, when God spared to Abraham the supreme test of his fidelity to the covenant.

Less dramatic, but equally significant, is the episode recorded in the fourteenth chapter of Genesis.[8] It describes the return of Abraham after his victory over the confederate kings who had raided the region of Sodom[9] and taken prisoner Lot, Abraham's nephew. Abraham was met by Melkizedek, king of Salem, in the Valley of Shaveh, glossed as "the King's Valley." The Jewish tradition has recognized in him a figure of the Messiah that was to come (cf. Ps 110:4) and the Church saw in him a type of Christ. The identity of this personage and his whereabouts are shrouded with mystery. It was tempting to identify Salem with Jerusalem, as does Psalm 76:2 and the quasi unanimous Jewish and Patristic tradition. The King's Valley is mentioned in 2 Sam 18:18, and Josephus volunteers the information that it was at a distance of less than twelve hundred feet from Jerusalem! Or is Salem the site bearing that name in the mountainous district east of Shechem? This would be more or less on Abraham's road, as he came back from his hot pursuit after the kings as far as the region north of Damascus. All that topography is of secondary importance for our present purpose. More revealing is the title "Priest of the God Most High," *El-'Eliôn,* given to Melkizedek. *'Eliôn* is not the proper name of the deity whom he serves, but rather a divine epithet qualifying the generic name for God, *El.* Note also the use of the word *kôhén* for "priest," a title not normally given to heathen priests, servants of the idols: these are called *kemârim,* an offensive word, which Luther's Bible renders in German by the otherwise untranslatable *Pfaffen.* The author of the Genesis fragment seems to think of a king-priest, such as some rulers in the pre-Semitic Middle East. In fact some vestiges of the sacral character of kings survived even in the Biblical writings in spite of the thorough expurgation to which they were submitted by the Temple scribes. Melkizedek brought out to Abraham offerings of bread and wine, blessed him in the name of *El-'Eliôn* and received from him the tithe of the booty recovered from the heathen kings. A Christian tradition saw in the *prosphorae* offered to Abraham a figure of the Eucharist. A relief panel in the cathedral of Reims shows the king-priest in the vestments of a Latin bishop, presenting the chalice to Abraham, who is dressed in a mediaeval coat of mail, and captions on images or postcards sold at the cathedral entitle the scene "the knight's communion," an unexpected sample of pictorial typology.

The real interest of the story, if we set aside its picturesque features, is that it opens vistas infinitely broader than the perspective of the covenant with Abraham, which was conceived in tribal terms, even though the tribes would some day be fused into an influential nation. But the priesthood of Melkizedek extends further out in time and space than the Aaronic priesthood, which was limited to the Hebrew people, and tied up to the existence of the Temple of Jerusalem, the ruin of which Jesus would announce: "There shall not be left standing stone upon stone" (Mt 24:2).

Commenting upon the story of Melkizedek, the Epistle to the Hebrews argues from it to prove the transcendence of the new economy with respect to the Old Testament (Heb 5:5-6, 6:20, and chapter 7, *passim*). When the author of

the Epistle, whether St. Paul or a disciple, writes of Melkizedek that he is "without father or mother or genealogy"
(Heb 7:3), his purpose is to make clear the superiority of
the eternal priesthood over the professional hierarchy of the
sons of Aaron, whose legitimacy depended on the accuracy
of lists painstakingly kept by the Temple scribes and remembered to this day, through family traditions, by those
of our Jewish neighbors whose surname is Cohen or Levy.
The messianic priesthood is forever, "according to the order
of Melkizedek" (Ps 110:4), before and after the Levitic
order, because "before Abraham was, Christ is," the First and
the Last.

The universality of his mediation is foreshadowed in the
very same stories which predicted the reunion of the covenanted tribes into a single nation. The Most High, of whom
Melkizedek was the priest, is the same God who revealed
himself to the Patriarchs at Beersheba,[10] the "Well of the
Oath" (Gen 21:31), as witness and guardian of the treaties
passed between the tribes and the inhabitants of the Negeb
with whom they came in contact. For his Providence extends
to all: Hagar, who fled into the wilderness, heavy with child,
was comforted by the "Angel of Yahweh," who announced
the birth of Ishmael, and the water from which she was
revived came to be known as *Be'êr la-haï rô'i,* "the Well of
the Living One who sees me" (Gen 16:13-14, variants in the
duplicate story Gen 21:9-21). The voice she heard was indeed
the voice of him who promised to the woman of Samaria the
"living water welling up to eternal life" (John 4:14).

CHAPTER VII

The Revelation to Moses

We have no intention to write here a biography of Moses
from his birth on the banks of the Nile to his death and
mysterious burial, nor a panoramic account of his times based
on the Biblical narrative and our ever-increasing historical information, nor again to trace the development of the Pentateuch by means of a critical examination of the text and its
presumed sources. A rudimentary knowledge of these should
be assumed from the start.[1] We aim rather at determining
the part played by Moses in the total process of the divine
revelation, and since the key to the understanding is Christ
himself, at discovering whether and to what extent we may
expect to hear his voice and discern his face in the reading
of the five Books traditionally bearing Moses' name. We
shall, therefore, approach our subject much as we did in
the preceding chapter with regard to the story of the Hebrew
Patriarchs.

The raw facts are as follows: the tribes of the Hebrews
designated by their eponyms, the twelve sons of Jacob, driven
by a period of drought and famine in Canaan, "descended"
into Egypt, where they were welcomed at first by a dynasty

of Pharaohs, presumably of Asiatic origin, who had seized power in the Delta and had established their rule over the entire land. The Hebrews settled in the land of Goshen, a district on the border of the eastern limit of the Delta, where they tended their flocks of sheep and goats. A number of them had found favor with the rulers of the country, and we see Joseph, one of Jacob's sons, in an important position in the administration of the kingdom. Traces of a certain acculturation can be found in the Bible. When Jacob died in Egypt, Joseph had the body of his father prepared by the Egyptian embalmers, that it might be brought back to the family tombs in the cave of Machpelah near Hebron (Gen 50:2-3). When he himself died, "being a man a hundred and ten years old, they embalmed him and he was put in a coffin, as they do in Egypt" (Gen 50:26).

When Moses appeared on the stage of history, the situation had radically changed: "There arose a new king over Egypt, who knew not Joseph" (Ex 1:8),[2] in consequence of a dynastic come-back of nationalists from Upper Egypt, who expelled the usurper kings and reduced to slavery the Asiatic elements of the population. Tradition has it that Moses, born in the tribe of Levi, rescued as a baby and adopted by an Egyptian princess but conscious of his origin and witness of the inhumane treatment of the Israelites at the hand of their masters, resolved, being come of age, to liberate his people. They fled, on a fateful night of Nisan, the first month in spring, the Egyptian host in hot pursuit after them; they forded miraculously the "Sea of Reeds" (Ex 13:18),[3] whose waters closed upon their enemies and drowned them all; they reached, after an adventurous march through the torrid canyons and gulleys of the Sinaitic peninsula, the lofty peak of Mount Sinai, which Yahweh had appointed for a rendezvous.[4] While the people camped in the little plain of er-Raha, Moses alone ascended the mountain, hidden from sight by ominous clouds, and received, in the mystery of the Presence, the charter which would make of the Israelites "a kingdom of priests, a holy nation" (Ex 19:6) or, according to the Greek version quoted by 1 Pet 2:9, a "royal priest-hood," βασίλειον ἱεράτευμα. God gave to Moses, written of his own hand, the ten commandments, and instructed him in the statutes, the ordinances relative to the cult, and the marching orders for the people toward the land which had been promised to the fathers and which, after ten years of wandering, they would finally conquer and occupy.

The narratives of the conquest describe the march toward Canaan as one single movement of the people as a whole; traces of partial operations, involving only parts of the tribes and allied clans, nevertheless can be detected in the text. A certain amount of schematization has taken place, which gives to the entire story the sweeping quality of an epic.

The above summary draws both on historical and legendary features. That a generous allowance should be made for the free treatment of the traditional material which the compilers of the Books had at their disposal, is not to be denied. A conclusive sorting out of factual and redactional or interpretive elements is nigh impossible and, as far as we are concerned here, futile. We deal with an icon, not with a photographic document.

Three themes stand out, of everlasting value, and germane to our purpose. The first theme is set in evidence in the episode of the burning bush (Ex 3:1-15). The time: when Moses, still a young man, suspect to the Egyptians in spite of his upbringing, had to flee for his life and take refuge among the Midianites, tribesmen of Northern Arabia, related by consanguinity to the descendents of Abraham. Some of their fractions roved about the Sinaitic peninsula with their meager flocks. Moses, now a shepherd, and having become the son-in-law of Jethro, a chieftain whom the Bible describes as "priest of Midian" (Ex 3:1), was favored by a momentous revelation from God, which gave him the sense of his destiny, and set the course of religious history for his people and for mankind. The place: the "mountain of God," Horeb, which a source of the composite narrative uses in synonymity with Sinai, which is preferred by the tradition of the southern tribes.

The Angel of Yahweh appeared to Moses in a flame of fire out of the midst of a bush; and Moses looked, and lo, the bush was afire, yet it was not consumed. And Moses said: I will make a detour and see that marvelous sight, why is it that the bush is not burnt? . . . But Yahweh said: Do not come nearer . . . I am the God of thy father, the God of Abraham, the God of Isaac, and the God of Jacob. And Moses hid his face, for he was afraid of looking upon God. Then Yahweh said: I have seen the affliction of my people. . . . I will send thee to Pharaoh, that thou mayest bring forth my people, the Benê Israel, out of Egypt. And Moses said unto God: Behold, when I come unto the Benê Israel and say to them, the God of your fathers has sent me to you, and they ask me, what is his name, what shall I tell them? And God said to Moses: I AM who I AM . . . And he said: Say this to the Benê Israel: I AM has sent me to you. . . . HE IS, the God of your fathers, the God of Abraham, the God of Isaac, and the God of Jacob, has sent me to you. This is my name forever, to be remembered throughout all generations.

A few words of explanation are necessary for the understanding of the Biblical account. To Moses, who had requested Him who was speaking from the bush to identify himself, God did not answer directly by telling his name but disclosed the mystery of his transcendent Being, what he had been to the fathers, and what he intended to be in relation to his people. The puzzling element of the entire section is the choice of the words, which the Hebrew text and, to a lesser extent, the versions followed by the entire Patristic tradition, interpret in reference to the meaning of the verbal root *h-y-h* (Hebrew), or *h-w-h* (Aramaic), "to be"; hence, in verse 14, "I AM who I AM," *éhyéh asher éhyéh;* "I AM has sent me to you." In the third person, I AM becomes HE IS, *Yihyeh, Yahweh.*[5] The Greek adds a metaphysical overtone which is not meant by the Hebrew, ὁ ὤν, "He who is." The answer to Moses' question, which sounds almost like a password, would, from now on, serve as a substitute for God's proper name. The Greek, therefore, will normally render Yahweh by ὁ Κύριος, and the Latin by *Dominus,* "the Lord." We need not wonder if, in Biblical sections relative to events preceding in time the revelation at the burning bush, "Yahweh" is already found in synonymity or even in juxtaposition with Elohim, ὁ Θεός, *Deus;* such anachronisms are frequent in texts resulting from the compilation of earlier popular traditions or written sources. Furthermore, a theophoric element akin to Yahweh, viz. *yahô, Yô,* and the like, appears in the composition of a number of personal or place names throughout the Semitic area. These names offer no clue to the etymology of this element. This affects but little the substance of the narrative in its revelational import.

The emphasis is twofold and amounts almost to a polarization. On the one hand, the absolute transcendence of the Holy One, his separatedness from everything created, is unequivocally affirmed. Only God can say, "I am," without any qualifier. It follows immediately that he cannot possibly be named by a human tongue, for a name necessarily defines and circumscribes, and God is the boundless and the uncircumscribable. We stand here on the threshold of what came to be known as apophatic theology, according to which no positive human concept can be formed of the divine Being, including the very concept of "being." We can speak of God only in negative terms, and meet him in the complete obscurity of the dark clouds which surrounded him on Mount Sinai. Maximus the Confessor describes therefore the perfect mind as the one "which, by true faith, has through supreme ignorance the supreme knowledge of the supremely Unknowable."[6]

The other pole is the involvement of God in the world of men. Paradoxically, it is because God is absolutely separated from the world that he is the Lord of history. He identified himself as the God of the Fathers, of Abraham, Isaac and Jacob. He who spoke from the midst of the burning bush is the same who had passed between the victims which Abraham had disposed in rows for a solemn covenant with God (Gen 15:9-18).[7] Thus was the alliance reaffirmed at the foot of the mountain. The voice that Moses heard speaking from the burning bush was properly God's Logos who, in the fulness of time, would be incarnate of the Virgin Mary and become man. Our iconographers have rightly inscribed the nimbus around the head of the Pantocrator with the three letters O Ω N.

Clement of Alexandria, familiarly discussing the proper

use of flowers, wreaths and crowns, raised the developments
of his *Paidagogos*—a third-century Emily Post for Alexandrian Christians—to the level of a mystical allegory: the
Father and the Son united in a common effort to save mankind, from the burning bush to the crown of thorns.

> I would also tell you another mystery. The almighty Lord of all,
> when he began making laws through the Logos and resolved to
> manifest his power to Moses, showed to him a luminous vision
> in the appearance of a burning bush; the bush was of a thorny
> kind. When the Logos rested from the work of a lawgiver and
> ceased to converse with men, then, mystically, the Lord was again
> crowned with thorns. Returning to where he had come down, he
> retraced up to the origin his descent of old. The Logos, visible
> at first through a bush, would again put on a thorny crown, to
> show that all this is the work of one power, the power of the only
> Son of the one Father and the principle and end of the Universe.[8]

A second theme initiated in the Book of Exodus and developed in the latter three Books of the Pentateuch, viz.
Leviticus, Numbers and Deuteronomy, is the theme of the
Law, originally given to Moses, and further interpreted and
implemented by jurisprudence in the course of Israel's national existence, until it would attain to the unchallenged
centrality which it occupies in posterior Judaism. Modern
Christians have some difficulty to understand the enthusiasm
of the Jews for the Law, and look askance on the merriment
which takes place on the day of *Simhat Torah,* "the rejoicing
at the Law," in the synagogues, especially those of Orthodox
Judaism.[9] We cannot help thinking, when we read the seven-
teenth *kathisma,* or when our Latin brethren psalmody the
Sunday hours, that the alphabetic Psalm 119, an encomium
of the Law, is terribly long and monotonous.

The Law appears to us an austere necessity, rather than
an occasion for rejoicing. We are inclined to regard legal
prescriptions as painful restrictions of our freedom, and
brakes to our spontaneity of expression or, at best, imper-
sonal gimmicks for maintaining social, cultural, or traditional
routines. That "best" easily degenerates into the worst legalism, in which the intention of the lawgiver is forgotten, and
the law becomes a blind rule rather than a paedagogy.[10] Ex-

ternal compliance turns into an easy way out of moral qualms, or escape from the tyranny of legalism is sought along various degrees of anarchy, from anomianism to antinomianism.

Obviously, these deformations are not to be imputed to the Law itself, but to a misconception and abuse of the Law. They had been denounced already by the prophets, and they would again be stigmatized by Jesus as the common sin of the Sadducees and the Pharisees, *inasmuch as* the former used the Law for political deals, and the Pharisees for ostentation and low-grade casuistry. Here I beg to insist on the word *inasmuch*. The fact that Jesus is vocal against these sins should not make us forget that he was the first who told to his disciples: "Render unto Caesar the things that are Caesar's" (Mt 22:21), and, condemning the hypocrisy of the Pharisees: "Do as they say, not as they do" (Mt 23:3). What he reproached to the Sadducees was their shady intrigues for prestige and power, not their efforts to safeguard whatever was left of national autonomy. What was damnable about the Pharisees was their pride, not their acriby, even though it may be deemed excessive in the observance of minutiae. Paul's disparaging appraisal of the works of the Law must be understood in the context of his argument against the Judaeo-Christians, not as a reversal of the total economy of salvation. The Western Reformers, in their denunciations of the abuses which had disgraced the Latin Church of their time, would recklessly follow suit to St. Paul's critique of legalism, and the ensuing controversy achieved the disintegration of the theological synthesis of the Middle Ages, by narrowing the concept of soteriology, and uprooting ethics from its doctrinal subsoil.

Our failure to understand the proper worth of the Law is that we conceive it as a categorical dictate: no reasons given, no reasons asked, in total abstraction of its origin and of its roots in the universal order. It was given according to the truth of creation and out of love, and it cannot possibly be obeyed otherwise than in truth and in love. Once more, we are brought back to the Trinitarian scheme as, crossing ourselves, we sing three times the verse of the Great Doxology: "Blessed art Thou, O Lord, teach me Thy statutes."

Nowhere perhaps in the Bible is the harmony of the legal order and of creation more strikingly expressed than in Psalm 19, where the themes of the heavenly bodies shining over the earth, and of the light of moral law, are indissolubly interwined. "The heavens declare the glory of God, and the firmament shows forth the work of his hands. The day unto the day tells of them, the night teaches them to the night. . . . Their voice went out through the earth, and their words to the end of the world" (Verses 1-4). Like unto those words, are the words of the Law, which is "perfect, reviving the soul, a sure testimony making wise the simple; rightful precepts rejoicing the heart, a command that is pure light to the eyes" (verses 7-8) as the light of the morning sun. "As a bridegroom he comes forth from his chambers, as an athlete eager to run the race, rising up from one end of the heavens in his circuit to the other end, and nothing remains hidden from its glow" (verse 5).

The tradition of the Church has rightly recognized in this athlete him who is hailed in the Canticle of Zechariah as the rising sun from on high (Lk 1:78). St. Ambrose of Milan, in a magnificent hymn used mostly in the Gallican liturgy, sings of the cock crowing through the night of Peter's denial, and of the first sunrays, all irradiated with the very light of Christ, which melted his heart unto repentance.

The miraculous subsistence of the Israelites in the wilderness is a third theme, perhaps the richest in allegorical interpretations, whether or not types of Christ in the strict sense. These have drawn the attention of early Christian exegetes and commentators. What is of particular interest for us is this: whereas the first two themes which we developed in the preceding sections of this chapter, namely the revelation at the burning bush and the giving of the Law, pointed to the identity of the Logos who would be incarnate as "the Christ" and would fulfill the Law in its letter and spirit, the episodes relative to Yahweh's providential care of his people during the march through the Sinaitic peninsula point, beyond the historical existence of Christ, to his abiding presence in the Church through the twin mysteries of baptism and the Eucharistic meal.

At each page we are reminded of water as a divine gift. For having wasted it wantonly and polluting it, we are suddenly made aware, perhaps too late, of its worth. The secret of underground sheets of water is hidden from men. When Moses led the Israelites back to Palestine, Yahweh himself revealed unto him the waters of Be'êr on the Transjordanian table land, and the Book of Numbers quotes the song— almost an incantation—of the well-diggers: "Spring up, O well! Sing ye to it, to the well which princes dug, which the nobles of the people delved with their scepters and with their staves" (Num 21:18). Water is life, and the narratives of Exodus never fail to mention all along the itinerary of the Israelites the points where they had been able to fill up their waterskins: the bitter waters of Marah, which Moses cured with a miraculous wood which Yahweh indicated to him (Ex 15:23-25);[11] the oasis of Elim, "where there were twelve wells of water and threescore and ten palm trees, and they camped near the waters" (Ex 15:27). When they murmured for thirst, Moses was ordered to "smite the rock, and there shall come water out of it, that the people may drink" (Ex 17:6). The fact that a similar miracle, possibly a duplicate due to the plurality of sources, is recorded in Num 20:1-11, brought the Rabbis to imagine, by way of explanation, that the miraculous rock followed the caravan of the Israelites, and St. Paul has adopted this curious piece of exegesis: "They drank from that spiritual rock that followed them, and that rock was Christ" (1 Cor 10:4).[12]

When the people, hungry and disgruntled, clamored for food, as they remembered the onions and fleshpots of Egypt and declared bluntly that freedom in a desert was no substitute for a full belly, God had given them the manna from heaven and flights of migrating quails, together with down-to-earth instructions to insure an equitable distribution, prevent hoarding, and make some provision for the Sabbath, when no collection of manna would be allowed. I confess that I am rather sceptical with regard to the tentative determinations, doubtfully relevant here, of the botanical phenomenon which may have given occasion to the Biblical narrative. One thing is sure: the water from the rock, the manna and the quails were not regarded as common fare, but as heavenly gifts. St. Paul stresses that the Israelites had eaten a spiritual food (πνευματικόν), drunk a spiritual beverage, gushing forth from a spiritual rock (1 Cor 10:4). On that basis, Christian tradition unanimously saw as many figures of our holy mysteries. "In older times, baptism had been in 'the cloud' and in the sea; but now, regeneration is through water and the Holy Spirit. Manna as a food was figurative, but actually the flesh of the Word of God is truly food, as He himself said: My flesh is meat indeed, and my blood is drink indeed."[13]

We are brought to a climax with the double feature Passover-Pascha. The Passover meal, *sêder,* is the commemoration in Jewish households, of the hurried supper eaten by the Israelites making ready for their departure from Egypt, in the night in which Yahweh slew the first-born of their oppressors (Ex 12:1-36). The Haggada for Pesah explains the details of the memorial celebration, in answer to the question asked according to tradition by the younger son: "Wherein is this night different from all other nights?" "We were Pharaoh's bondmen in Egypt, and the Lord our God brought us out therefrom with a mighty hand and outstretched arm . . . the Holy One, blessed be He, in his glory and power."[14] The *sêder* is a meal of the wayfarers parting with the past, and an anticipation of the future: "To Jerusalem, the coming year!"

The exhortation and intercessory prayer of Jesus in chapters 13-17 of the fourth Gospel follows this line: Jesus takes leave of his disciples, commits them to his Father, as he departs from this world for the everlasting kingdom which he is going to inaugurate by his redemptive death and resurrection. And it is in this spirit that the Twelve took place around the table set for the Passover meal, at the urging of the Master: "I have desired of a burning desire to eat this Passover with you" (Lk 22:15).[15]

The Old Testament festival of Passover had incorporated earlier elements of a pastoral and agricultural observance:

the sacrifice of the yearlings, incidentally a link with the typology of the sacrifice of Isaac, and the offering of the first ears of wheat of the season, both rituals being reinterpreted and loaded with a new symbolism, the lamb hastily slaughtered and roasted, and the unleavened bread, the *matsoth,* of the Exodus night.[16] Realizing all the figures, the Eucharistic meal around the Christian altar is the memorial of the sacrifice of Christ, and an anticipation of the future "till he come." Pauline tradition and the synoptic Gospels, by stressing the sacrificial aspect of the Eucharist, are by no means in contradiction with the Gospel of John, which omitted the description of the supper, but recorded extensively the words of farewell of Jesus to his disciples and, beyond them, to us all. It so happened that the night in which he was betrayed saw the last *sêder* and the first Eucharist.

The complex typology of the revelation to Moses and the events of the Exodus may be compared to a row of icons, representing spiritually the mysteries of the inaugurated kingdom and the reality of the aeon to come. We stand before the iconostasis. Open the royal gate, pull aside the curtain, then we shall see the altar, the *artophorion,* Christ the conqueror.

CHAPTER VIII

Royal Messianism

Before we address ourselves to the subject announced by the title of this chapter, a preliminary remark is necessary, in order to dispel a common illusion regarding the historical status and theological significance of the Hebrew monarchy. We tend to assume that the period of the kings, historically the peak of Hebrew history, expresses best its essence and true meaning, supposing as we do that history has a meaning. A glance on the chronological tables given in English Bibles, the Jerusalem Bible for instance, proves instructive with regard to this gratuitous assumption. It dates the first entry of Abraham in Canaan toward 1850 B.C., close to two thousand years before the final destruction of the Temple of Jerusalem in A.D. 70. David is reported to have conquered Jerusalem toward 1000 B.C., and this approximation marks the real starting point of the monarchy. It collapsed definitively in the summer of 587 B.C., 134 years after the fall of Samaria in 721 B.C., the interval being one of desperate struggle for survival on the part of the kings of Judah. The arithmetic is quite simple: 413 years of monarchic rule versus a total of 1920 years of existence of the Hebrews as a distinct historical and religious group, followed from A.D. 70 onward by the Judaism of the Diaspora, including the creation of the present Israeli state.[1]

But the problem is not merely one of dates. We are impressed by the unusual density and consistency of the information provided by Biblical sources during the era of the Hebrew kingdoms, whose chronicles yield abundant material susceptible of being critically processed in view of writing a history of Israel synchronized with extra-Biblical data, such as documents and monuments of the ancient empires of the Near and Middle East. By contrast, the task which the critical historian faces when dealing with the post-exilic period is unusually arduous, due to the fragmentary character of the sources, the discontinuity of the information, and the variability of the literary patterns used by the compilers. The simple picture we would like to draw of the Hebrew monarchy would be misleading on account of its superficiality.

The redactional composition of the writings describing the period between the Exodus and the establishment of the monarchy, roughly from 1250 to 1000 B.C., may help us in a certain measure to become aware of the complex historical significance of the Hebrew period of the kings. The Books of Joshua and Judges record traditions relative to the conquest and occupation of Canaan by the Israelites. The origin of these traditions often can be traced with reasonable probability either to the group of the northern tribes—Israel— or Judah in the south. The Book of Joshua has built them into an epic of the conquest. The Book of Judges, concerned with the relations which developed afterwards between the Israelites and the Canaanites, disposed the various episodes of their friendly or stormy coexistence in a conventional framework similar to that of the *toldoth* in Genesis, proceeding by units of forty years, multiples or fractions thereof.[2] Another characteristic of Judges is the theory of an automatic collective retribution in the manner of Deuteronomy, based on the double equation: faithfulness = prosperity, sinfulness = disaster.[3] Similar principles of composition can be detected in the first Book of Samuel, which describes the "pre-history" of the monarchy in Israel, showing forth the radical opposition of two tendencies, respectively favorable or hostile to the royal institution.

The century following the conquest of Palestine by Joshua brought about radical changes in the social status of the Israelites. The semi-nomadic shepherds would grow roots in the soil of Canaan and turn peasants and agriculturers. The tent-dwellers would settle in villages grouped into rural districts. The cohesion between the tribes, imposed by the strategic necessities of the conquest and of the early years of occupation, would gradually be relaxed. The country had been overrun and the Canaanites defeated in open battles, but they held out in cities which Joshua had been unable to conquer.[4] After the bloody encounters of the first hour and a few episodes of local character, a *modus vivendi* had prevailed; threats to peace came principally from outsiders, Asianic invaders, tribesmen from Arabia and Transjordan, the Philistines of the Mediterranean seaboard, against whom the Israelites eventually would make common cause with their Canaanite neighbors. The entire period was one of decentralization and assimilation. The unity of the nation had been forged in the desert, around the Ark of the Covenant between Yahweh and his people, but now Yahwism was threatened by the popular appeal of the local sanctuaries of Ba'al.

In cases of pressing danger from without, charismatic leaders would rise up in the name and spirit of Yahweh, the so-called "Judges,"[5] rally the tribes or groups of tribes and repel the enemy until the next crisis. The failure to cope with the infiltration of the Philistines in the central district of Ephraim, the destruction of the Israelite sanctuary of Shiloh and the capture of the Ark, which the Philistines exhibited as a war trophy in the temple of Dagon in their city of Ashdod (1 Sam 4:11, 5:1-2), dealt the last blow. Some way of restoring the moribund cohesion of the tribes had to be found and made to work without delay. The Israelites sought the solution of the problem in the establishment of a central monarchy, under a king, "like the other nations." There had been precedents. Abimelech, the son of Gideon, the Judge who had delivered the strongly Canaanized district of Shechem from the Midianites, Amalecites, "and all the *Benê Qédem*" (Jdg 6:33), had himself proclaimed king with the support of the Canaanite burghers of the city, who financed the enterprise by a levy on the treasury of the temple of the Ba'al berith (Jdg 9:1-6). The adventure aborted, but its memory lingered in the northern districts when, after Solomon's death, they broke away from Judah and proclaimed Jeroboam king over Israel.

The first real king over the entire nation is Saul, whom Samuel, the last of the Judges, anointed at the request of the people, under the threat of an invasion by the Ammonites who, toward the same time, had built themselves up into a local kingdom on border of the Transjordanian tableland. The compilers of the Books of Samuel have tried, not too successfully, to harmonize two traditions relative to the monarchy of Saul. According to one of their sources, Samuel had warned the people of dire consequences if they persisted in calling a human leader to lord it over them, an exacting master and a tyrant against whom they would have no recourse (1 Sam 8:10-22). Another source[6] regarded the institution of the monarchy not as a concession on the part of Yahweh, who would reluctantly give in, but as meeting his positive approval, in view of the critical situation and in accordance with the general trend of the history of that period.

At any rate, the institution of a monarchy by popular demand was a departure from genuine Hebrew tradition, as it was substituted for the theocratic ideal of the Fathers. Yahweh himself had manifested himself to them and pledged his unfailing support on the sole condition of faith and obedience. Yahweh had led them, under Moses and Joshua, into their inheritance. By what amounted to a transfer of title, the benefits of the covenant sworn to Abraham and renewed on Mount Sinai, would be reported on the head of the king anointed to reign in God's name over his people and lead them to their destiny. The history of Israel had entered the age of royal messianism which, in its historical form, is but a phase bracketed within God's total economy of salvation.

The relative unification of the people under the scepter of Saul had somewhat relieved the external pressure, but the internal situation was chaotic. Saul understood unity as the hegemony of his own tribe of Benjamin, surrounded himself with a body of men chosen for their physical strength and prowess (1 Sam 14:52)—he himself was, "from the shoulders and upward, higher than any of the people" (1 Sam 10:23). He had no other political principle than the application of brute force, vindictiveness and suspicion, as he was subject to fits of insanity attributed to an evil spirit which possessed him by intermittence, until his dismal downfall.

In reality, the monarchy began with David, the head of an enduring dynasty, the history of which comes to us through the flamboyant accounts of David's heroic lifetime (1 Sam 16:1 to 1 Ki 2:11), the magnification of Solomon's years (1 Ki ch. 3 to 11:43) and, beginning with the secession of the northern tribes (1 Ki 12:1 ff), the chronicles of the two kingdoms officially kept by the royal scribes, and which were the sources used by the compilers of the Books of Kings and the Books of the Chronicles.[7] The tie between the Davidic dynasty and the messianic conceptions of the Jews was such that, long after the ruin of the dynasty, David became the type of the Messiah that was to come in the person of Jesus Christ. Hence the motif of the "Tree of Jesse," David's father, as a popular iconographic translation of the genealogical scheme.

David: a lad from Bethlehem; a page at the court of the king, who conceived a fierce hatred against him out of morbid jealousy; a fugitive in the desert of Judah, where the king's men pursued him without respite. He became a popular figure, both feared and admired by the people on account of the guerilla warfare which he conducted successfully with his band of outlaws; daring, resourceful, loyal to his friends and, against every expectation, against his persecutor whom, on an occasion complacently described by the narrator, he could have killed by surprise at the mouth of a cave in the desert of Engedi; but, said David, "The Lord forbid that I should stretch my hand against him, seeing that he is the Lord's anointed" (1 Sam 24:6). All in all, he cuts the figure of a good sheikh, as they go. After Saul's suicide following the defeat at Mount Gilboa (1 Sam 31:4), the tribes chose David for king. He reigned seven years and six months in Hebron, the religious center of the tribe of Judah, keeping watch over the tombs of the Patriarchs. His master stroke as a strategist and a politician was the conquest of Jerusalem, which he made his capital and where he reigned for thirty-three more years (2 Sam 5:1-10). Jerusalem had thus far remained in the hands of the Jebusites, a Canaanite clan, and could not be claimed as integral part of any of the tribes. According to the Book of Joshua, the limit between Benjamin and Juda passed "on the southern shoulder of the Jebusi" (Jos 15:8), leaving Judah to the south and Benjamin to the north. By its location, Jerusalem was eminently apt to play the part of a "federal district" between the two rival groups of tribes. David exploited the situation to the utmost, not, however, without resistance on the part of the separatists from the northern tribes, which he did his best to rally, but which seized eagerly any pretext to intone a seditious refrain: "We have no part with David, no inheritance with the son of Jesse; each one to his tents, Israel!" (2 Sam 20:1, cf. 1 Ki 12:16). They had even tried to capitalize on the intrigues of Absalom, David's rebellious son. The king had to flee temporarily from his capital; the revolt was eventually repressed and the opposition driven underground. The Books of Samuel, reflecting the Deuteronomic image of the ideal king and echoing the voice of the prophets, interpreted the misfortunes of David as a temporal punishment for a moral failure. In a flare of passion for Bathsheba, the wife of one of his officers, Uriah the Hittite, he had treacherously sent the husband to his death by having him ordered "to the forefront of the hottest battle," during the operations of siege against Rabbath Ammon (2 Sam 11:15), a crime which he expiated dearly. According to Jewish tradition, Psalm 51, "Have mercy on me, O God . . . my sin is ever before me," was attributed to David "when Nathan the prophet came to him because he had gone in to Bathsheba."

It belonged to Solomon, the son born of "her who had been the wife of Uriah" (Mt 1:6), to consolidate the unity precariously achieved by his father David. The dynasty reached its peak during his lifetime. His personal gifts of wisdom and justice, his genius in domestic and foreign affairs, and the brilliancy of his reign are described in the first Book of Kings as a vision from the Arabian nights. The kingdom was redistricted, in view of a political and fiscal centralization. Diplomatic and commercial relations were established with the major foreign powers. Palestine assumed what should have been its proper function in the development of the Near and Middle East: forming a bridge between Egypt and the Asiatic empires, a link between the Mediterranean West and the regions east of the Red Sea, in cooperation with Arabian caravan leaders and Phoenician seamen. Able successors might have brought under control the excessive fiscal charges made necessary for Solomon's enterprises, the construction of Temple, palace, and military bases, but Roboam, heir to Solomon, did everything to exacerbate the people, rebuked their legitimate grievances, and precipitated the ruin. The kingdom of David and Solomon fell apart, and slowly, but surely, the Promised Land became the battlefield of rival empires.

We have now to count with two Hebrew kingdoms: Israel in the North, Judah in the South, most of the time in conflict with each other, seldom engaged in a common enterprise, and this eventually with disastrous results, shifting their political or military alliances with neighboring states, and playing a reckless game of diplomacy with the super-powers: the Mesopotamian empires and Egypt.

Our sources of information for the history of the northern kingdom are unfortunately lacunous and for the most part adversely biased. Apart from the testimony of archaeology and the *ostraca*[8] discovered in the royal cellars of Samaria, where jars of wine, oil and grain were stored by the tax collectors, with indication of the fiscal district to which they were credited, all we know is secondhand, from the records of the Jerusalem scribes who compiled the Books of Kings, and who refer explicitly to the annals of the two kingdoms, interpreting the Israelite records from their own southern point of view.

Materially speaking, the North had a distinct superiority in numbers, especially if one counts the districts of Eastern Manasseh across the Jordan. Its cultivable acreage and the general quality of its soil exceeded those of Judah, which had to live on the semi-desertic pastures and the rocky terraces of its vineyards and olive groves. The open border districts in the northern part of Israel made for easy relations with the Aramaeans of Syria, not an unmixed blessing from an ethnic and religious point of view. The major handicap of the northern kingdom was the number of dynastic changes it suffered, being repeatedly shaken by palace revolutions and military coups.[9] The "House of Omri," however, achieved a reasonable degree of stability, and was followed, after the murder of Joram by Jehu (2 Ki 9:24), by a line of rulers among whom Jeroboam II registered the longest reign, forty-one years, in the kingdom of Israel.

Until the foundation of Samaria by Omri, the northern kingdom had no capital that could rivalize with Jerusalem. Jeroboam had been proclaimed at Shechem and he fixed his residence at Tirzah, in the highlands north-east of Shechem. The religious center, distinct from the political capital of the kingdom, was Bethel, which could prevail itself from the memory of Jacob's dream (Gen 28:11-22) and as such could attract pilgrims, but could hardly counteract the attraction of Solomon's Temple, even though the holy place boasted the high-sounding title of a "royal sanctuary, a foundation of the kingdom" (Amos 1:13). The Biblical records present the religious observances of Bethel as schismatic innovations defiled by compromission with Ba'alist cults. As a matter of fact, the "innovations" may have been at least in part a return to local practices different from those prevailing in Jerusalem. At any rate, the prophets who denounced these practices looked upon them from quite a different angle. What they condemned was rather the abuse of ritualistic formalism and the hypocrisy of the people on both sides of the border.

The kingdom of Judah was numerically weaker and

poorer, but this inferiority was redeemed by the homogeneity
of its population. Judah was less open to foreign influences
than the northern kingdom. Apart from a few notable exceptions, the purity of its faith and of the official cult was
better sheltered against contamination. Jerusalem, the Davidic
capital, and Solomon's Temple, made for cohesion and stability. Hebron welcomed pilgrims to Mamrê and to the cave
of the Machpelah, the resting place of the Patriarchs. The
stability of the dynasty was endangered only once, by the
wholesale murder of the sons of Ahaziah. However, the ac-
cession of Joash, who had escaped providentially, was not
challenged, and the young king was accepted by acclamation
(2 Ki ch. 11). Yet the glory of the reign of Solomon was a
thing of the past, and his imperial dream, a nostalgic memory.
Several kings were partly successful at stabilizing for a time
the deteriorating condition of the state, but they failed to
reverse the downward trend. Hezekiah, for instance, took
effective measures for defending his capital against an imminent siege by the Assyrians. His efforts were recorded with
admiration by the annalists of the kingdom (2 Ki 20:20; 2
Chr 32:4-5, 30), and were remembered by the Siracide in
his panegyric of the great men of his nation (Eccli 48:7).
It remains to be seen, however, whether the failure of
Sennacherib to conquer Jerusalem was entirely due to
Hezekiah's preparatives,[10] to the sudden epidemic which
decimated the Assyrian forces, or to the fact that Sennacherib
was urgently recalled to his capital to quench a rebellion of
his Babylonian subjects, all plausible reasons bracketed together irrefutably under the rubric of an act of God's Providence in favor of his people.

Religious reforms were undertaken by several monarchs:
Jehoshaphat, Hezekiah, Josiah, who called the Judaeans to
a fuller observance of the Law and who restored the Temple
worship defiled by unwarranted innovations. Under the majority of the reigns, however, "the high places were not re-
moved," and, often with the participation of the king, the
people continued to offer sacrifices and incense on the hills,
and under every green tree (2 Ki 15:4; 16:4), so deeply

ingrained in the mentality of the people were the practices of the Ba'alist cults.

Even under the best kings, foreign policy, under the threat of invasion by the eastern empires, could be disastrous. It should suffice to recall here the stupidity of Hezekiah showing his treasures, his arsenal and his storehouses to an envoy of Merodach Baladan, the champion of the Neo-Babylonian cause against the Assyrians (2 Ki 20:12-19), or the tragic end of Josiah, falling on the battlefield of Megiddo, where he engaged Neko, who was ascending from Egypt to join forces with the Assyrian king against a Neo-Babylonian uprising (2 Ki 23:29-30; 2 Chr 35:20-25). The collapse was inevitable. Samaria had fallen in 721 B.C., its population had been deported *en masse* and replaced by foreign colonists. Judah succumbed in 587 B.C.; the Temple was destroyed, the kingdom's aristocracy and upper middle class exiled to Babylon, and the country left in prey to anarchy.

How would the Israelites cope with the disaster? The people were in exile or scattered abroad among the nations, in the various *diasporae.* The Davidic dynasty, which had the Promise, was finished as a dynasty. A triumphal restoration of Solomon's grand design was out of the question; a universal gathering of Abraham's children under a Messiah ruling in the name of Yahweh was not to be dreamt of. The problems of reconstruction after the euphoria of the return from exile under the Persians confronted the leaders with a dilemma: how to open the terms of the antique covenant in order to face a situation which had never been known before, and, on the other hand, how to preserve the faith and the traditions of the Fathers in the midst of the indifference or the hostility of the Gentiles and of the defectors from Judaism?

An earthly king would no longer reign in the land, and the regime of the community would be inspired again by the theocratic ideal of the origins. The early prophets had regretted its disparition when the monarchy was instituted and when Yahweh gave in to the request of the people. Ezekiel refers to a personage whom he calls the *Nasî',* "the prince,"

"His Highness," from the root *n-s-'*, "to exalt," "to lift up." The title had been used unspecifically by the late compilers of pre-exilic traditions, and it is found, with the meaning of community leader, in documents of the post-exilic period. The *nasî'* is not a king, his title implies no ritual anointing; it is found on a coin of Bar Kokbâ, in the time of the second revolt against the Romans: "Simon, *nasî'* of Israel."[11]

The evolution of the messianic idea is nowhere more clearly perceived than in the history of the Temple. Solomon had built it to be the house of Yahweh. The first Book of Kings (ch. 6-7), describes a compound of buildings: the "House" and its courtyards, where the people met, and, to the south, the royal palace, on the triangular hill which had been the acropolis of the Jebusites and where David had established his residence.[12] Solomon's successors frequently had encroached upon the traditional prerogatives of the college of priests, by increasingly regarding the Temple as a palatine chapel, or by making arbitrary and sacrilegeous innovations, like Ahaz, who had a new altar built on the model of the altar of the temple of Damascus and who altered the ritual (2 Ki 16:10-18), or like Manasseh, who erected altars "for all the host of heaven in the two court-yards of the house of Yahweh" (2 Ki 21:4-5, cf. 2 Chr 33:4-5).

After the destruction of Solomon's Temple, Ezekiel, about to describe the Temple of the future, uttered, under divine inspiration, the angry words of Yahweh: "The place of my throne . . . where I will dwell in the midst of the Benê Israel forever . . . shall the house of Israel not defile any longer, neither they, nor their kings, in their setting of their threshold by my threshold, of their post by my posts" (Ezek 43:7-8). Ezekiel's project is entirely dominated by the dogma of God's transcendence. The successive courtyards through which one would gain access to the esplanade where the sacrifices are offered, were designed to filter the worshippers according to the degree of their consecration to Yahweh. Only the priests might enter the House, where, behind the veil of the sanctuary, Yahweh resides, invisible, between the Cherubim. This would be the principle followed by the architects of the

Temple of Herod, from the precincts of which Jesus expelled the money changers and the venders of doves for the sacrifices, and where a low chancel marked the extreme limit beyond which no Gentile was allowed.[13]

The dream of royal messianism in its temporal version remained in the consciousness of the people as an elusive mirage, a pretext for insurrection against foreign rulers, or as the positive appeal of a higher and broader ideal. One hoped, against hope, for the advent of the leader who would mete justice to all, bring peace to the world until eternity would close in, subdue the oppressors, and receive the homage of the mighty, a new Solomon to whom the kings of Sheba and Seba, the sea-lords of Tarshish and the isles, would pay tribute (Ps 72).[14]

The prospect of Psalm 72 is long-range. Psalm 110 is a close-up: "Oracle of Yahweh to my Lord" (*le 'adôni*); "my Lord," the king anointed, who shall sit on the right of the Sovereign Judge, who shall be sent to rule over his enemies in the power of God, for he was begotten before the history began, "in the womb of the morning," "a priest forever after the order of Melkizedek." He purchased his judicial authority at a price, "drinking of the brook in the way," the brook of affliction, which his ancestor David had to cross when, repulsed by his own, he had to flee from his capital (2 Sam 17:22).[15]

The editors of the Jerusalem Bible note that Christ realized to the letter the oracle of Psalm 110. This is correct, but an understatement. To the Pharisees who sought to involve him in contradictions, Jesus opposed the testimony of the Psalm. His retort remains implicit, but it silenced his adversaries, and it is clear to us. According to the flesh, he is the descendent of David, but as the eternally begotten, he is the Lord of David, the Messiah who was to come, thrice anointed, king, priest, and prophet.

We have tried to show how the messianic theme had to be liberated from compromission with the ways of an earthly monarchy. Not until it underwent the necessary transpositions would it be realized in history, in the person of Jesus Christ. These successive transpositions will be the subject of the following chapters.

CHAPTER IX

Immanuel, God with us

If the face of our Christ really shines through the shadows of the Old Testament, we would expect the prophetic writings to be the privileged locus of this manifestation, inasmuch as the ministry of the Old Testament prophets was consummated and recapitulated in the prophetic office of Christ, and because the prophecies of the Old Testament point invariably toward him.

A prophet is commonly understood as a person endowed with a supernatural gift of foreseeing and foretelling future events. This is true enough, but it is only a part of his function. A few words may be useful at this point as an introduction to the present chapter and the following two.[1] The Hebrew term *nâbî*, a nominal form from the Semitic root *n-b-'*, designates primarily "one who is called."[2] His mission is to declare the will of God to his fellow men, to reveal God's secrets, and to announce what shall come to pass. Thus he is a seer and a divinely appointed herald. The author of the Books of Samuel explains that the *nâbî* was formerly called in Israel a "Seer" (1 Sam 9:9).[3]

The prophet does not act of his own initiative. He is

called by God, and that call is irresistible: "The lion has roared, who will not fear? The Lord God has spoken, who can but prophesy?" (Amos 3:8). Jeremiah wished to elude God's command, "but the Lord said unto me: Say not, I am a child; for thou shalt go to all that I send thee, and whatsoever I command thee, thou shalt speak. . . . And the Lord said unto me: Behold, I have put my words in thy mouth" (Jer 1:7-9). The historical books of the Bible refer to what appears to have been guilds of professional *nebîim* (plural of *nâbî*), playing musical instruments and prophesying (1 Sam 10:5, 10-13). Elisha figures as the higoumen of a brotherhood of prophets (2 Ki 4:38) and, being in the retinue of Jehoram, king of Israel, allied with Jehoshaphat against Moab, he requests that a harpist be brought in, in order that "the hand of the Lord came upon him" (2 Ki 3:15). Rhythm and melody may well increase the receptivity of the prophet, but there will be no prophecy unless "the Word of the Lord comes unto him." There is no such thing as self-induced prophecy, which could not be but imposture or the voice of the Evil One.

A servant of the Word, the Old Testament prophet is more than a preacher depending on his knowledge of the Scriptures and on his skill as an expositor. He is God's agent, fully empowered: Jeremiah is set by God "over the nations and over the kingdoms, to root out and to pull down, and to destroy and throw down, to build and to plant" (Jer 1:10). The acts of the prophet, as well as his words, have a sacramental meaning, an effective virtue. When the prophet Ahijah tears his cloak into twelve pieces, ten for Israel, two for Judah [and Simeon], the schism of the tribes, painstakingly united by David, is more than foretold (1 Ki 11:30-32). When Jeremiah breaks an earthenware jar in presence of the elders and the priests, they are made to understand that the shattering of the nation has begun. The sentence has been pronounced and cannot be reversed (Jer ch. 19).

St. Jerome wrote of Isaiah that "he should be called an Evangelist, rather than a prophet" since "you would not think that he is prophesying about the future, but that he is composing a history of the past."[4] A prophet he certainly is, by every token. He describes his vision, as the Lord manifested himself to him in the Temple of Jerusalem and gave him his orders: "In the year that King Uzziah died—it must have been in 767 B.C.[5]—I saw the Lord sitting upon a throne, high and lifted up, and the train of his mantle filled the Temple. . . . Then I said, Woe is me, for I am undone, because I am a man of unclean lips, and mine eyes have have seen the King, the Lord of hosts!" A seraphim, taking a glowing coal from the altar, "laid it upon my mouth and said: Lo, this has touched thy lips, thine iniquity is taken away and thy sin is purged" (Is 6:1-7). The Orthodox priest, wiping his mouth with the veil after partaking of the precious blood, repeats the very same words which were spoken to Isaiah: "This has touched my lips, and shall take away my iniquities and cleanse me from my sin."

Christian Tradition is unanimous in proclaiming Isaiah the "Prophet of the Incarnation." Our liturgical readings draw heavily on the canonical Book of Isaiah,[6] which we can regard as the paradigm of prophetic literature since, more than any other book of the Old Testament, it points to the birth and mission of Immanuel, to the passion and triumph of the Messiah, and to the Christ of the latter days.

Isaiah's early prophetic utterances are oracles of woe, denouncing the social disorders which threatened the kingdom of Judah in the latter half of the eighth century B.C., a time when the rich grew richer and the poor poorer, when the leadership was failing or corrupt, the priests greedy and arrogant.

> Woe unto them that join house to house, who add field to field until there is no more space and until they are the sole owners of the land. Woe to them that rise early in the morn, to run after strong drink, and who tarry late at night, till wine inflames them. . . . Woe unto them that draw iniquity with cords of falsehood. . . . Woe unto them that call evil good and good evil, that put darkness for light and light for darkness. . . . Woe unto them that are wise in their own eyes and shrewd in their

own sight. Woe unto them... who acquit the guilty for a bribe,
and deprive the innocent from his right (Is 5:11-23).

A few years earlier, Amos, the rude shepherd of Tekoa,
had rebuked the magnates of the northern kingdom. His
invectives were especially vehement against the wealthy
matrons of Samaria.

> Hear this word, you cows of Bashan, who are in the mountain
> of Samaria, who oppress the poor, who crush the needy, who say
> to your husbands: Bring, that we may drink. The Lord has sworn
> by his holiness that, behold, the days are coming upon you, when
> they shall take you away with hooks, even the last of you with
> fishhooks (Amos 4:1-2).

Such sins cry to heaven. Offerings for sin, solemn rites of
expiation, will be of no avail as long as the heart is not
changed, for Yahweh cannot be bribed, like their corrupt
judges.

Isaiah was an aristocrat, at ease at the court and among
his peers of the gentry, "a noble man," writes St. Jerome,
"of urbane elegance, without the slightest tinge of rusticity
in his discourse."[7] Amos was an uncouth shepherd and
migrant farm laborer, irked by the luxury of the ivory
halls of Samaria (Amos 3:15) and the pompous nullity of
the chief priest of Bethel (7:12). But we would be dead
wrong if we regarded either of them as demagogues. They
did not speak of their own, but Isaiah was sent to harden
the heart of the people (Is 6:10);[8] Amos was taken from
behind the flock and ordered to prophesy (Amos 7:14-15).
Thus it is the Word of God we hear through their words,
the same Word who was made man and who chastized the
blind leaders of his people, who denounced the opportunism
of the priests and the formalism of the Pharisees, hypocrites
who "shut up the kingdom of heaven against men," "devour
widows' houses," make their converts "children of hell,"
perjure themselves by swearing through the altar, pay the
tithes on trifles, but neglect "judgment, mercy and faith,"
observe the fine points of the ritual, but desist not from
being extortioners; they are white-washed sepulchers full of
every rottenness, great builders of memorial monuments, "to

hide the bodies of the righteous whom they have defrauded"
(Mt 23:13-29). The message is the same, and Jesus did not
tune it down.

The first major division of the Book of Isaiah contains
among other pieces three closely related oracles which have
been regarded unanimously in Christian circles as messianic.
They revolve around a mysterious personage named program-
matically Immanuel (*'immânû-El*), "God with us."[9] The
historical setup is as follows: the kings of Damascus and
of Samaria are leagued against Judah, whose king Ahaz
they try to dethrone. His isolationist policy in the face of
an Assyrian threat is regarded by them as high treason, and
they set out to attack Jerusalem, whose inhabitants grow
panicky. Isaiah's purpose is to reassure Ahaz and the people
who, trembling before their hostile neighbors and, either
through ineptitude or heedlessness, do not seem to realize
that they will be next in the path of the Assyrian invaders.
And here is a sign of immediate reprieve which the prophet
brings, unsollicited, in the name of Yahweh: "The *'almah*,
ἡ παρθένος, is with child and shall give birth to a son
whom she will call (or, in the Greek, thou wilt call, καλέ-
σεις) Immanuel. The child will not yet be able to tell bad
from good, and already the lands of the two kings who
threaten you shall have been laid waste" (Is 7:14-16).

Shall we understand that Isaiah announces a sequence of
events of which the former, viz. Immanuel's birth, serves
merely as a chronological indication that the latter, viz. the
fall of Damascus and Syria, will follow soon? Or is the
emphasis on the unusual character of the birth, as one might
surmise from the fact that the prophet had offered a sign,
declined by Ahaz, "from the depth of Hades or from the
heights above," regions equally inaccessible to humans?
Early Christian writers were prompt to remark, like St.
John Chrysostom, that if the Immanuel was not born of a
virgin, there would not have been any sign.[10] Theodoret:
"If the birth was no virgin birth, but from carnal union,
how then, since it would then have followed the course of
nature, was it heralded as a sign?"[11] The argument is not

absolutely conclusive. The Hebrew *'almah* generally means a young woman, actually married, or of marriageable age. The Greek παρθένος seems more precise: a virgin, and if so, the event in question is not only the first of a chronological sequence, but a miracle as well. The precision, however, is slippery, for there is no lack of examples of παρθένος being said of girls who are not virgins, but of maiden-like appearance.[12] It remains that the *'almah*, with the article, both in Hebrew and in Greek, is set in prominence as a definite person, presumably well-known in court circles.

The identity of Immanuel poses similar problems. Ancient Jewish traditions identified him with Hezekiah, Ahaz' son and successor. In that case, the prophecy was the mere announcement of the birth of a crown-prince within a matter of months. But this interpretation raises chronological difficulties, already discussed by St. Jerome, and which modern investigations of Biblical records do not resolve but rather accentuate.[13]

We have no way of knowing for sure who, in the eyes of Isaiah's contemporaries, were the *'almah* and Immanuel. The prophecy certainly made some sense at the time, inasmuch as, counting from the birth of Immanuel and adding a few years, the defeat of the two "firebrands" announced by the prophet would be consummated. For us, the *dramatis personae* have value of types and the reality they typify can be understood only in the light and from the vantage point of the Christian revelation. The *'almah:* Mary. That which is conceived in her from the Holy Ghost and born in Bethlehem of Judaea: Jesus, who shall save his people from their sins. "Now all this took place, writes St. Matthew, that it be fulfilled that which the Lord had spoken by the prophet: behold, the virgin[14] shall conceive and bear a son, and they shall call his name Emmanuel, which is to be translated: God with us" (Mt 1:23). For Isaiah, a hope and a prayer; for us, the actual reality of the Incarnation.

A second oracle, which can be dated as posterior by a few years to the *'almah* prophecy, is no longer occasioned by the panic of the citizens of Jerusalem, who have recovered from the attack of the Syrians and the Israelites of the northern kingdom. It is worded as a hymn of thanksgiving for the marks of protection which God gives to his people. The future is still uncertain, but there are enough grounds for hope at long range.

> The people that walked in darkness have seen a great light; they that dwell in the land of the shadow of death, upon them has the light shone.... For unto us a son is given, and the government shall be upon his shoulder, and his name shall be Wonderful, Counseller,[15] the Mighty God, the Everlasting Father, the Prince of Peace. Of the increase of his government there shall be no end, upon the throne of David and upon his kingdom, to order it and to establish it with justice from henceforth, even forever (Is 9:2-7).

The oracle is prefaced by a recollection of the calamities suffered by the populations of Galilee during the Assyrian forays of the late ninth and the early eighth century B.C. I see no compelling reason for dissociating the prologue in prose, "In the former days, he humbled the land of Zebulun..." (Is 9:11) from the oracle in Hebrew verse, to which it constitutes a perfectly valid introduction, no matter when or by whom it was written. The historical context is clear. Seen from Jerusalem, the threat of the Syro-Ephraimite neighbors, defeated and conquered by the Assyrians, has been definitively averted. But another threat materializes. The Assyrians, who by now control Damascus and Samaria, make ready for the kill. Judah is alone. Hezekiah is more inclined to listen to his foreign agents and his military advisers than to heed Isaiah's messages. Anyway, it is too late. Punishment for the sins of the nation can no longer be evaded. But in the midst of these shadows, the prophet intones his hymn of light. It is no longer the announcement of an immediate reprieve as in the *'almah* prophecy, but a far-sighted prospect. After things will have come to the worst, there will be, within the boundaries of human history, a restoration based on the certainty of God's promise.

The oracle is messianic and Davidic-dynastic. The child heralded by a protocol of royal names, indeed more than royal, even if we make the most lavish allowance for Oriental hyperboles, can hardly be someone else than the Immanuel whom, after all, we have not been able to identify at the eighth-century level.[16] If so, the child born of the *'almah*, whoever he was, has become a type of the prince who, some day, will restore David's throne to its 'pristine splendor. But we are no longer in the zone of proximate, foreseeable events. As it reads, the oracle, with its verbs in the *perfectum propheticum,* does not permit any reckoning by years or by number of generations.

Once again, the Old Testament Scriptures propose a riddle, to which no decisive answer can be found unless we turn to the Gospels and to the Tradition of the Church. The king that is given to us is Christ himself. The festal Menaion appropriately prescribes the reading of Isaiah's oracle of the royal names for the ninth hour on the eve of the Nativity, and some Latin breviaries, for the first lesson of the Christmas nocturns.

We have described the oracle of the royal names (Is 8:1-7) as Davidic-dynastic. The messianic perspective opened by the third great oracle in the Immanuel section, namely 11:1-9, is emphatically futuristic.

> And there shall come forth a shoot from the stump of Jesse, and a branch shall grow out of its roots. Upon him shall rest the Spirit of Yahweh, spirit of wisdom and discernment, spirit of counsel and might, spirit of knowledge and fear of Yahweh (Greek: spirit of knowledge and piety, εὐσεβείας, and he shall "breathe"[17] the fear of Yahweh) (Is 11:1-3).

Whereas the massoretic Hebrew of verses 2b and 3a is confirmed by the Qumram text of the Book of Isaiah, the Greek translation, followed by the Latin Vulgate, may have used a different Hebrew prototype or interpret the difficult lesson of 3a so as to add a seventh spirit to the three pairs enumerated in verse 2. At any rate, the prophecy is clear: the future king issued from the root of Jesse, David's father, shall be endowed with the fulness of the Spirit of God, the Spirit who was upon Moses and his elders (Num 11:17, 25), upon the Judges (Jdg 3:10; 11:29), the Spirit who "clothed" Gideon (Jdg 6:34), who spoke through the mouth of David the prophet-king (2 Sam 23:2). The sacred oil with which the Messiah will be anointed is but the symbol of the Spirit of God who shall rest upon him and make him "with righteousness judge the poor, decide in equity for the meek of the earth, smite the earth with the rod of his mouth, and slay the wicked with the breath of his lips" (Is 11:4).

We have by now left the contingencies and mediocrities of the Hebrew dynasties, and of all dynasties and governments for that matter. All the metaphors of court etiquette are exploded. We come close to the Pentecostal oracle of Joel, "My Spirit over all flesh" (Joel 2:28), which St. Peter will appropriate without any transposition (Acts 2:16-18). Then will justice and peace prevail in Zion, "for the country shall be filled with the knowledge of Yahweh, even as the waters swell the sea" (Is 11:9). The new age is described with cosmic amplitude, bursting through national boundaries and temporal conditions. It is a return to Eden, harmony among men; the symphony of man and nature, once broken through revolt, will be fully restored (Is 11:5-8).

The dream of the prophet is no longer one which can be realized on earth, but only on the new earth and in the new heaven which shall be. We have left the space of men, and our "re-entry" is contingent upon the appearance of him who is to come, and of whom the spiritual king of Isaiah is but the type.

Our Christ is an authentic descendent of David, from the root of Jesse. He "dwelt among us," on the earth of men. When he was baptized in the Jordan by the Forerunner, "The heavens were opened, and he saw the Spirit of God descending like a dove and alighting on him, and lo, a voice from heaven saying: this is my beloved Son, in whom I am well pleased" (Mt 3:16-17). The testimony of the Father gives authority to the inaugural statement of Jesus in the synagogue of Nazareth when, opening the scroll of the prophets, he read from the Book of Isaiah: "The Spirit of the Lord is upon me, because he has anointed me to preach the gospel to the poor, he has sent me to heal the broken-hearted, to preach deliverance to the captives and recovery of sight to the blind, to set at liberty them that are bruised, to proclaim the acceptable year of the Lord. . . . This day is this Scripture fulfilled in your ears" (Lk 4:18-21). The final act of God's economy is still ahead of us; as a man, Jesus was not given to know the day or the hour. He has ushered in the kingdom of God, but the kingdom, which is not of this earth, awaits consummation in power. Then will the entire course have been run, from the garden of Eden, to the "Passover" into the "heavenly paradise"[18] foretold by the prophet, when the mission of the Pantocrator is accomplished, and when the time of history shall yield to eternity.

CHAPTER X

Servants and the Servant

Modern scholars call chapters 40-55 of Isaiah the "Book of the Consolation of Israel," a denomination appropriately drawn from 40:1. This section contains among other fragments four outstanding poems in which there appears the mysterious figure of a "Servant" (*'ébéd*), to whom God has assigned a prominent role in the reconciliation and restoration of mankind. In the first poem (42:1-9), Yahweh introduces the Servant and gives him his order of mission.

> Behold my servant, whom I uphold, my chosen one, in whom my soul delights. I have put my Spirit upon him; he shall bring justice to the nations. He will not cry or lift up his voice or make it heard in the streets. A bruised reed he will not break, the smoking flax he will not quench, he shall bring forth judgment unto truth. He shall not fail nor be crushed till he has established justice on the earth, and the islands wait for his law. . . . I, the Lord, I have called thee in righteousness, I have taken thee by the hand and formed thee,[1] and I have given thee for an alliance with the people, a light to the nations.

In a second poem (Is 49:1-6), the Servant himself describes his calling and quotes the words of Yahweh, who sent him to be a Savior to Israel and the nations.

113

Listen, O isles, unto me; hearken, you peoples, from afar. Yahweh called me from the womb; from the bowels of my mother has he called my name.... And he said unto me: Thou art my servant, O Israel, in whom I will be glorified. I said to myself: I have labored in vain, spent my strength for nought. Yet surely my right is with Yahweh; my reward, with God. And now, Yahweh has spoken, who formed me in the womb to be his servant.... It is too small a thing that thou shouldst be my servant to raise up the tribes of Jacob and to restore the survivors of Israel. I will give thee for a light to the nations, that my salvation may reach to the end of the earth.

Verse 3 poses a problem, inasmuch as the Servant, who is described in verse 1 as a physical person, is identified in verse 3 with Israel, which appears in verse 6 not as servant, but as beneficiary of the work of the Servant. An ingenious solution was offered by the late Professor Dhorme.[2] Yahweh sees in the Servant the eminent representative of the people who shall be saved, the true Israel, "recapitulated" in the Servant.

The Servant appears again in a third poem (Is 50:4-11), in which a preview is given of the many ordeals which he will have to face in the fulfilment of his mission.

The Lord Yahweh gave me a tongue of disciple, that I may know a word to sustain the weary. Morning after morning he wakes up my ear, that I may hear, as the disciples do. The Lord God has opened my ear, and I was not rebellious, I turned not backward. I gave my back to the smiters, my cheeks to them that pulled out my hair. I hid not my face from outrage and spitting. The Lord God will help me; I shall not be confounded, for I have set my face as hard as flint, and I shall not be put to shame. He is near, who will justify me. Who will contend with me? Let us stand together! Who is he, who would be justified against me? Let him draw near! Behold, the Lord God will help me; who then shall condemn me?

The poem concludes with an exhortation to all men, whether Gentiles walking in darkness, or God-fearing Jews, to heed the appeal of the Servant, to lean upon God, whose enemies shall be consumed by the fire which they themselves have lighted.

The climax is reached in the fourth poem, which proclaims the final triumph of the Servant, bought at the price of violent persecutions heroically endured (Is 52:13 to 53:12).

Yahweh first announces the ultimate vindication of the Servant whom he designates to the people as if he were pointing to him with his finger, even addressing him in the second person (52:14). Then the people comment on the dramatic career of the Servant and its outcome (53:1-11), and the conclusion is drawn by Yahweh himself. We shall give the entire piece, following the Hebrew text as closely as possible—it is uncertain in places—the ancient versions offering some divergent readings, which we have eventually adopted.

Yahweh: Behold, my Servant shall prosper, be exalted, lifted up, raised very high. Multitudes were appalled at seeing thee![3] Disfigured beyond human semblance, he looked no more like a son of Adam, but he shall startle many nations. Before him kings shall shut their mouths, for they will see a thing they were not told, and learn something unheard (52:13-15).

The people: Who has believed that which we were made to hear, and the arm of Yahweh, to whom was it revealed? He grew like a shoot before him, a root out of dry ground. He had no beauty, no brightness that we should look at him, no appearance that we should desire him. Despised, abandoned of men, a man of affliction, visited by sickness, as one before whom we hide our face,[4] despised and of no account to us. Truly he has borne our sickness and carried our afflictions. We had counted him stricken, smitten of God and afflicted. But he was stabbed for our transgressions, crushed for our sins. The chastisement that makes us whole was upon him, and with his stripes we are healed. All of us, like sheep, have gone astray, every one his own way, but Yahweh has caused the sins of us all to fall upon him. Being oppressed, he humbled himself, he did not open his mouth. Like a lamb that is led to the slaughter, like a ewe, dumb before her shearers, he opened not his mouth. From detention and judgment he was taken away. His destiny, who cares about it?[5] For he was cut off from the earth of the living; for the transgression of his people he was stricken (the Greek adds: to death). They gave him a grave with the wicked, and with the rich[6] in his death, although he had done no wrong, nor was there any deceit in his mouth. But it was the will of Yahweh to crush him. Yahweh afflicted him with sickness. If Thou makest his soul an offering for sin, he shall see his offspring and prolong his days, and the good pleasure of God shall thrive under his hand. For the travail of his soul he shall see [light][7] and shall be filled.

Yahweh: By his knowledge, my righteous servant shall make many righteous, and their iniquities he shall carry. Therefore will I give him a portion among the great, and with the mighty to share the booty, because he has stripped himself unto death and was counted among the transgressors, he who bore the sin of many and who intercedes for ôthe transgressors (53:1-12).

It should be observed here that the locution "Servant of Yahweh" does not appear in any of the four poems, but that it is a convenient stereotype used by modern exegetes, on the basis of 42:19b: "Who is blind like my pledgee,[8] dumb as Yahweh's servant?" As a matter of fact, several servants not identifiable with the Servant of the poems appear in the "Consolation of Israel." At any rate, the historical background is obvious. Judah has succumbed, and its elite has been exiled to Babylon. A prophet arises in the Spirit of Yahweh and announces the certainty of a return into the homeland. It cannot be Isaiah himself, who is by that time dead and buried. He seems to have fallen in disfavor with the court and, according to Jewish traditions, he would have been put to death under Manasseh.[9] The chronological perspective is not in focus. Some fragments in the Book of Isaiah present the deliverance as imminent; some others, presumably introduced at a later date into what I would like to call the Isaian corpus, look to the latter days for an implementation of God's design for his people.[10]

A similar incertitude due to a multiplicity of planes in the development of the prophecy had already been observed in the Book of Immanuel, ranging from imminent, to distant but foreseeable, to indefinite future. The inspired author of the "Consolation of Israel" seems to be perfectly conscious of a mutual relationship between historical happenings chronologically distant from each other and of which the former condition, announce and typify future events according to God's Providence. The author or authors of Isaiah ch. 40-55 outline nothing less than the economy of the prophetic mode of revelation. Thus, the calling by name of Cyrus (Is 45:1), points to an act of God, by which the promises made *of old* to Abraham, "my friend" (41:8), will be realized *tomorrow*. Only Yahweh can possibly do this, because "I, Yahweh, the First (*rishôn*), I, with the latter ages (*'eth-aharônim*), I am He!" (41:4). And the argument is further confirmed in verses 21-23a, in which the gods of the nations are challenged to show forth their titles.

> State your case, says Yahweh. Produce your arguments, says the King of Jacob. Let them step forward and tell us what will happen. The former events, what were they? Tell us, and we shall make up our minds. Let us know what is going to happen after these, or what is going to pass thereafter; and then, we shall know that you are Gods (Is 41:21-23).

The author of the Consolation of Israel distinguishes two sets of events: ancient ones, which have been realized, and prophecies, which are being announced here and now in correlation with the former, and whose realization will prove their authenticity. Thus 42:9, in conclusion of the first Servant song: "Behold, the former have come to pass; the new ones I do announce; before they sprout up, I make you hear them." And here is precisely the sin of the people, that, having witnessed the realization of older prophecies and hearing the new ones, they still remain incredulous (48:3-8).

The identification of the Servant poses methodological problems similar to those regarding the identity of Immanuel. The list of plausible characters has been dressed by C. R. North.[11] The very length of the catalogue might lead us to conclude, irreverently, to the impotence of an exegetical method based exclusively on the textual criticism of the Old Testament. A few short remarks, germane to our purpose, should suffice at present. Job: to be sure a suffering just man, helpful to his fellowmen and concerned about his children, but he was not "called," he did not understand why he was suffering, and whatever we know of God's secret design on him, we know through the "Prologue in heaven." Moses: a leader and lawgiver, but no expiatory victim. Isaiah: a herald and, according to some tradition, a martyr, but that did not make him the principal agent of a general redemption. Uzziah, the leper king: in a sense, a type of him "before whom we veil our face" (53:3), but the similarity is of a mere episodic nature: Uzziah did not "bear the sin of many"

(53:12); rather he died a lonely death, confined in his house, and was buried in the burial field of the kings, but not in the royal sepulcher (2 Chr 26:23). Hezekiah: a tolerably good king, but whom Isaiah had to rebuke sharply for his politicking. Josiah and Jehoiachin, who saw the kingdom being liquidated; how then could they be credited in any way with preparing the restoration foretold by the prophet of the Consolation? Jeremiah: he suffered a great deal and complained loudly; the Servant "opened not his mouth"; Jeremiah was a victim of what has been described as the occupational hazard of a prophet of doom,[12] but he is not a sacrificial victim. Ezekiel: a comforter of his fellow exiles, dreaming of reconstruction and author of a blueprint for the restoration of the Temple, a project which died on the drawing board. The Deutero-Isaiah, i.e. the prophet of chapters 40-55, whose identification with the Servant of the poems has been seriously considered,[13] does not seem to be the Servant any more than Isaiah was Immanuel, or the "prophetess," the *'almah;* the words of the Servant in the second and the third poem are quoted *by* the prophet, they are not the prophet's words. Cyrus, "my anointed,"[14] is *a* servant, he is not *the* Servant (Is 45:1-3). Zerubbabel: an efficient organizer and reconstructionist, but can we really recognize in his modest achievements the transcendent role to which the Servant was called? As for the few post-exilic worthies at the end of the list, they have very little indeed to command our attention.

A number of modern commentators, especially in Jewish circles, have tentatively identified the Servant not with a physical person, but with collective entities, such as the prophets, the priests, the historical or the ideal Israel, the righteous, the remnant that shall return. These identifications however, are so vague that they are practically worthless or even misleading. For example, no matter how exalted the priestly caste may have appeared in the eyes of the exiles in Babylon, it is difficult to see in its members a body of martyrs, whose martyrdom would be vindicated in triumph, or to expect a prophet to proclaim one of their number as the Servant *par excellence.* Furthermore the Servant, as we have already observed, cannot be identical with those whom he comes to serve; his mission is "to bring back Jacob, and gather Israel" (Is 49:5), and whether the Servant is a person or a body of people, he must be formally distinct from those he is called to save.[15]

Of course, there is no lack of passages in the Consolation of Israel where the people itself is, explicitly or implicitly, regarded as Yahweh's servant. But Israel-servant is not the Servant of the poems; in one of those passages (Is 42:18-19), it is rather the opposite: "Hear, you deaf, and look, you blind, that you may see. Who is blind but my servant? or deaf as my messenger whom I sent? Who is blind as my pledgee,[16] deaf as Yahweh's servant?" This is not to say that the persons, physical or moral, listed above, had absolutely no part in the realization of Yahweh's plans, but it is clear that none of them embody in themselves all the features attributed by the poems to the Servant *par excellence.* There is always something lacking, and something essential.

A majority of modern exegetes, bent upon satisfying the requirements of the historical method, would search for the literal meaning of the Servant poems and of the second part of the Book of Isaiah as a whole, in the perspective of contemporary Jewish, or more precisely, Judaean expectations, in fulfilment of the covenant with Abraham and the promise made freely to the House of David for a time unspecified, but within human history. The latter clause, however, leaves unexplained or insufficiently explained those passages in the Consolation of Israel, including the Servant poems, which suggest a complete spiritualization of the national aspirations, and something more than the mere repatriation of the exiles. These passages reveal a divine economy out of proportion with a lawyer's understanding of the letter of the covenant, and call for a radical transposition of the "dispensation in figures."

The commentators who shy away from launching forth beyond a tight historicism are apt to declare that modern scholarship can no longer recognize any signification beyond the immediate meaning of a given passage of Scripture understood in its philological-historical context, and to denounce what they regard as a feedback from later traditions, or an intrusion of Christian theological speculations into the science of hermeneutics. We cannot resist the temptation to quote at this point, to the risk of being charged with the crime of lèse-academia, a sharp retort of Origen against pedestrian commentators of his time, who caviled about the meaning of an obscure passage of Exodus: "O you, perpetual scholars from childhood to old age, studying always and never attaining to the knowledge of truth! Don't you understand that those sayings are prophetic? If you wish to understand, you can do so only through the Gospel."[17]

We have no intention of disparaging the efforts of modern scholars trying to determine what the Servant poems meant to the Jewish exiles of the sixth century B.C. However, the search, thus far, has not exhausted the content of the poems, and the identity of the Servant remains elusive. The prophet, beyond the immediate or proximate contingencies of Jewish history, had a vision exceeding all temporal and spatial limitations, which challenges the adequacy of positive exegesis. The texts are prophetic, and the key to the prophecy is to be found, willy-nilly, in the Gospel of the New Testament. The final identification of the Servant is with Jesus Christ, sent, suffering, triumphant. Conversely, the clear message of the Servant poems gives the first indication that the death on the cross is a sacrificial death, and not a meaningless, scandalous episode.

We readily admit that Christian interpreters often were carried further than sober hermeneutics would tolerate. The abundant quotations from the "Passion" of the Servant in the Gospel narratives of the Passion of Our Lord, and the readings from Isaiah in the liturgical services of both the eastern and the western churches for Great and Holy Friday often caused the faithful so to associate the Old Testament type with its realization that they thought of the description of the Servant's Passion as of a fifth Gospel. In the Latin Church the *Improperia,* which are sung on Good Friday prior to the Mass of the Presanctified, add to the verses from the Servant poems other texts such as Isaiah 5:4, and Psalm 22 (LXX and Vulg. 21). And had not Christ himself appropriated the opening words of the Psalm when, dying on the Cross, he cried aloud *"Eli, Eli, lama sabachtani, that is to say, My God, my God, why hast thou forsaken me?"* (Mt 27:46; Mk 15:34)? As critical a scholar as Professor Norman Snaith goes even so far as to declare that Christ "deliberately modeled his life on the Servant of the Lord. He saw himself as the Servant."[18] This is undoubtedly an extreme statement (Nestorian-flavored) from which adventurous conclusions are being drawn to explain the so-called policy of messianic secret and the silence of Jesus during his trial.

It is commonly agreed that the Gospels, rather than being didactic expositions of the faith, reflect the proclamation of the "Good News" to the crowds and in the church assemblies. Popular preaching had to capture the imagination of the masses, and this may explain the insistence of the Evangelists on the correspondence of some episodes of the Passion with specific details of the Old Testament prophecies. The following list is given merely for the sake of illustration. Matthew 26:31 and Mark 14:27: Jesus foretells the defection of the apostles, cf. Zechariah 11:12-13 (not Jeremiah, as Matthew has it erroneously). Matthew 27:35, Mark 15:24, Luke 23:34, John 19:23: the soldiers casting lots for Jesus' garments, cf. Psalm 22:18. Mark 15:27-28: Jesus led to the Cross with two criminals, cf. Isaiah 5:12. Matthew 27:48, John 19:29: the sponge filled with vinegar, cf. Psalm 69:21. John 19:36: "a bone of him shall not be broken," cf. Exodus 12:46. John 19:37: "They shall look on him whom they pierced," cf. Zechariah 12:10. Matthew 27:57ff, Mark 15:46: the tomb of the noble Joseph, cf. Isaiah 53:9.

Less striking in appearance are instances in which the Gospel writers argue from Old Testament texts, for example St. Matthew quoting extensively Isaiah 42:1-4, in the first Servant poem, (Mt 12:18-21): "Behold, my servant, my chosen one. . . . I have put my Spirit upon him, he shall bring

justice to the nations..." Or St. Paul, addressing the Jews
and quoting from Isaiah 49:6, in the second Servant poem,
(Acts 13:47): "I have set thee to be a light to the Gentiles,
that thou shouldst be for salvation unto the ends of the
earth." The "Great Epistles" have drawn their doctrine on
the atonement from passages in the fourth poem which
cannot, short of prejudice,[19] be interpreted otherwise than as
stating clearly the vicarious suffering and death of the Servant
of Yahweh: "Truly he has borne our sickness" (53:4-5),
and "If thou makest his soul an offering for sin" (53:
10b-12).

The sufferings of the Servant should never be considered
apart from his triumph, which gives meaning to them in
retrospect, nor do they result in the vindication of the Servant
alone, but in the redemption of those for whom he has
suffered.[20] This was never overlooked in the traditional interpretation of the Church or in her choice of readings and
excerpts for Holy Week. It is truly the face of Christ we
contemplate in the figure of the Servant, who "through death
trampled death, and restored life to those in the tombs."

CHAPTER XI

Christ of the Latter Days

The prophetic literature during and after the Exile shows forth a remarkable transformation. After the preaching of moral and social Yahvism by the prophets of the eighth century, and after the announcement of immediate or proximate retributions to be visited upon the entire nation, prophetic voices among the exiles, now that the monarchy was destroyed and the dynasty extinguished, had begun to tell of a restoration of Israel in terms of a theocracy and of an open-ended messianism, lifted up above the earthly conditioning of political history. The post-exilic writers and late Judaism acknowledged this transformation of the prophetic theme and the passing of an ancient mode of revelation.

To the faithful living under the Old Testament, the absence of prophecy, or prophecy becoming scarce, was an ominous sign of being abandoned by Yahweh, as if he refused to communicate with them any further. The author of the Books of Samuel, describing the religious and cultural let-down of the ancient theocracy which the intermittent rule of the Judges had been unable to prevent, had already noted how "the word of Yahweh was rare in those days, the vision not widespread" (1 Sam 3:1). For the prophet Micah, the absence of prophecy would be a deserved punishment for the sins of the people: "Night upon you, no more vision!" (3:6). Psalm 74:9, which is a lamentation on the ruin of the Temple: "Signs we see not, there are no prophets any more," or Lamentations 2:9, "No more Torah; the prophets receive no vision." The Books of the Maccabees insist, without comment, on the cessation of the prophecy in their time. No decision could possibly be taken for rebuilding the altar of burnt offerings defiled by the soldiers of Antiochus Epiphanes "until a prophet speaks" (1 Mac 4:46), but there are no more prophets! The oppression had no equal since the day "when a prophet had spoken last" (1 Mac 9:27). Simon Maccabee, after his victory over the Syrians, obtained the Principate and the dignity of High Priest by common consent to the day, unforeseen, "when a trustworthy prophet, προφήτης πιστός, would appear" (1 Mac 14:41).

Seen from the vantage point of our Christian faith, the fact that the post-exilic prophecy was on the wane and that soon no prophetic voice would be heard any more, is one feature of the general economy of divine revelation. The Jewish people had to be weaned. The time drew near when the Logos of God would become man and speak to men without intermediary. The last prophet, and "more than a prophet" (Mt 11:9), would be John the Baptist, who pointed to Jesus,[1] unless we count as prophecy the words of Caiaphas, that Jesus should die for the nation (John 11:51), "an iniquitous verdict inspired by impiety, which the event proved actually true and turned into a prophetic utterance."[2]

Some literary factors make it eventually difficult to trace the evolution of the concept of prophecy, for the prophetic books are by no means systematic, homogeneous records, the specific character of which we might ascertain at a glance, but compilations of oracular messages delivered in diverse circumstances and at various times by a prophet or his disciples and continuators. To these must be added fragments inserted at a later date by an editor who regarded them as germane to the original message, plus erratic blocks which found their way into the text for some obscure reason.

The Book of Isaiah, which we have precedently chosen as paradigm and whose text was stabilized early,[3] abounds in such occurrences. Some late fragments were inserted among earlier poems composed during the Exile and even among the Immanuel oracles, as if Isaiah himself were dreaming ahead and envisioning a universal return to the earthly Paradise. Similar observations could probably be made on the basis of other prophetical writings, for instance the Book of Jeremiah and cognate literature, namely Jeremiah proper (Hebrew and Vulgate), the text of Septuagint, Baruch, the Lamentations, and the so-called Epistle of Jeremiah. The fact, however, that the connection of these diverse writings with the prophet was assumed on shakey critical grounds rather than on a clear thematic kinship, may account for the fact that the compilers of the Bible have chosen to leave the elements of a hypothetical Jeremiah corpus separate and unedited.[4] These critical problems must be kept in mind as we work our way through the late prophetic literature and as we try to discern the face of Christ in the uncertain dawn which preceded his advent in the flesh.

Our Bible reading has taken us thus far through two of the three ages of messianism. The first was the age of pre-messianism, the Protevangel and the Patriarchal history, beginning with the calling of Abraham, Yahweh's friend, "in whom all the nations of the earth shall be blessed" (Gen 18:18), prior to whom Christ *is* (John 8:58), unto whom the Father could raise up worthy sons from "these stones" (Mt 3:9), to take the place of an ingrate and unruly nation.

The second age is the age of royal messianism. He who is to come shall be born of David's blood. In days of dynastic crisis or of national emergency, the prophets had warned the Israelites against presumption and overconfidence, and they did not veil the unpopular truth that the promise of a Savior from the House of David meant no exception from the impending disaster, brought upon them by their callousness, their disregard for personal or social ethics, and by the inept politics of their kings.

The historical setup for the third age of messianism, following the defeat of the nation and the years of the Babylonian Exile, was one of reconstruction. A minority of the exiles—the greater number had emigrated or were comfortably established in the land of their captors—returned to Palestine following the decree of Cyrus (583 B.C.). They found their homesteads occupied by the *'ammê-hâarâtsoth*, a medley of low-class Judaeans, Samaritans, Philistines and Edomites. The precariousness of the resettlement and the problems faced by the returning exiles should in some way be familiar to us, in our age of economic instability, class struggle, displaced persons and discharged veterans. The explosion of Hellenism gave the signal for the final act of the drama. From now on, the Jews would be confronted with a dilemma: either fight and work in the apparent collapse of any dynastic hope, rebuild the territorial integrity of the nation, or else reinterpret the message of the prophets and seek the realization of their dreams beyond the horizon of this world. Yet an issue was found in history: one day, the star of the Magi led true believers "to thee, Bethlehem Ephrata, not the least among the clans of Judah, for from thee shall come forth one who is to be ruler in Israel" (Mic 5:2 and Mt 2:6).

It was a religious motivation which drove the deportees back to Jerusalem, for "how could we sing the canticle of Yahweh in a strange land?" (Ps 137:4). Cyrus, an instrument in Yahweh's hand, had made possible the return to Zion. It was hailed by the prophets as a second Exodus, "like in the days of thy coming out of the land of Egypt" (Mic 7:15). Yahweh himself would lead his people along the paths in the desert, miraculously made straight and level, "that Israel might safely walk with God's glory" (Bar 5:7-9). The hyperbolic description of the triumphal march exceeds by far what the most optimistic could possibly expect (Is 49:9-13). Also (Is 40:3-5): "A voice cries: Prepare in the wilderness a road for Yahweh!" Are we still treading the dusty, sandy, stony trails of the eastern desert? The Evangelists, quoting the prophecy from the Septuagint, have understood that the voice was that of the Baptist, calling sinners to repentence for meeting the Messiah (Mt 3:3 Lk 3:4). A chain of types is evident here: the first Exodus, out of Egypt, through the Sea of Reeds; the second Exodus, out of Babylon, through the desert; the Forerunner pointing to Jesus as he set out to walk along the roads of Palestine, preaching and healing, ascending to Jerusalem, unto the Cross and the Resurrection.

Once in the homeland, at grips with the dark realities of the resettlement, the most urgent task of both the priests and the prophets was to prevent the repatriates from regretting the more-than-tolerable conditions of life which they had created for themselves, through their own tenacity and industriousness, in Babylon and in the Diaspora. The problem was to make them accept the hardships of the reconstruction in a ruined land and among hostile usurpers. The spiritual appeal of the pre-exilic and exilic oracles needed to be stepped up. It had become a pressing necessity to fight disillusionment and discouragement. The returning *gôlah,* a collective appellation for the deportees as a body of persons, which came to be used as a title of honor, ought to be a holy *gôlah,* a resurrected people. This was no new concept. It was part of the requirements of the Torah: "You shall be unto me a kingdom of priests, a holy nation" (Ex 19:6). This obligation is still upon us, inasmuch as we are the New Israel (1 Pet 2:9).

The absolute demand made by the prophets, interpreters of the covenant, would certainly not support the contention of some Zionists that the modern Israeli state is, as such, the historical realization of the promise to the Fathers. A state operating on secularized political and economic principles may not easily claim its birthright under a covenant based exclusively on faith in the divine revelation.

The latter part of the Book of Isaiah, chapters 56-66, is marked by the recurrence of three major themes, often intertwined. The first one is the elevation of the ethnic concept "Israel" to the superior status of an ideal community, in fulfilment of its providential destiny. Jerusalem is not a mere cluster of houses of stones and mortar, destroyed by the Chaldaeans and painstakingly restored under Nehemiah, but it shall become the spiritual capital of a regenerated nation.

In token of her consecration, Jerusalem is given symbolic names, which are as many programs: "City of Righteousness, Faithful City" (Is 1:26). "City of Yahweh, Zion of the Holy One" (Is 60:14). "City of Truth, the Holy Mountain" (Zech 8:3). Some of the new appellations are reminiscent of Hosea 2:23. The inhabitants of Jerusalem shall be "a people of Holiness, Yahweh's Redeemed" (Is 62:12a). Their walls and gates shall be called "Salvation" and "Praise" (Is 60:18). A new altar is erected in the main courtyard of the Temple, to replace the venerable structure destroyed by the Babylonian invaders; the perpetual holocaust is again offered morning and evening, and the votive sacrifices are resumed (Ezra 3:3). Nehemiah scouts by night the perimeter of the city (Neh 2:12-16), organizes the workers for the reconstruction of the ramparts (Neh 3:1-32); and the people celebrates the solemn dedication of the walls and gates to the singing of the psalms and processional hymns (Neh 12:27-43).[5]

Yet the holy *gôlah* was not immune against the temptation of declining, through lassitude, from their high resolve. The initial wave of enthusiasm was not enough. A radical change of heart was needed, and this would be God's greatest gift to his people: "I will take the stony heart out of their flesh and I will give them a heart of flesh... and they shall be my people, and I will be their God" (Ezek 11:19-20). This oracle of the prophet is God's answer to the prayer of the Psalmist: "Create in me a clean heart, O God, and renew a right spirit within me. . . . A broken and contrite heart thou wilt not despise" (Ps 51:10, 17). Only in total compliance with the demands of the prophets will a restoration make sense, for then, and then only, "wilt thou delight in right sacrifices, in burnt offerings and holocausts, and bulls shall be offered on thine altar" (Ps 51:19).

The requirements of the priestly ritual and the moral demands of the prophets must be taken in their complementarity, inasmuch as a spiritual revival is the condition *sine qua non* of true worship and since, on the other hand, the Temple observances were the normal framework for the religious life of the people. The near-to-puritanical observances of Nehemiah (13:19-21), were meant to safeguard the purity of the faith and the right observance of the Mosaic Law against all threats of contamination. The urging of the prophets Haggai and Zechariah, allowing no rest to the people until the Temple be fully restored and the cult reestablished, is not to be interpreted as a move back toward religious formalism, but as the best means to preserve the moral and social consciousness of the community. It is in relation to this Old Testament background that the words of Jesus must be understood when, resting near the well of Jacob, he said to the Samaritan woman: "The hour comes and now is, when the true worshippers shall worship the Father in spirit *and* in truth" (John 4:23).[5] We underscore the word "and," for no disjunction is permitted here. Men are not pure spirits, but creatures of flesh and blood; the balance is to be kept in obedience to the full truth, and not to be sought in a false freedom, where "everything goes."

A second theme develops perspectives of which the Deutero-Isaiah had only given previews. The messianic offer of salvation will be extended to portions of mankind outside the boundaries of the chosen people, for Yahweh is indeed the God of the Universe and will eventually be recognized by exotic nations, Egypt and Ethiopia, as their deliverer (presumably from their Persian conquerors) and the only true God.

> Thus speaks Yahweh: The husbandmen of Egypt and the traders of Kush,[7] the Sabaeans, men of stature, shall come over to you, and they shall be yours, they shall follow after you, in chains they shall come over and bow down before you and beseech you. God is with you only and there is no other god beside him. Truly thou art the hidden God, O God of Israel, Savior....

> There is no other god except me, a just God and Savior. There is
> none beside me. Turn to me and be saved, all the ends of the
> earth, for I am God, and there is none other (Is 45:14-22).

These affirmations are repeated in the prose which opens
the third part of the Book of Isaiah, clearly of post-exilic
age, since it supposes that the order and the rules of the
Temple worship have been regularly resumed.

> Thus says Yahweh: the eunuchs who keep my sabbaths, choose
> what pleases me, and hold fast to my covenant, I shall give them,
> in my house and within my walls, an everlasting name, which
> shall not be cut off, and the foreigners who unite themselves
> with Yahweh . . . these I will bring to my holy mountain and
> make them joyful in my house of prayer. Their burnt offerings
> will be accepted on my altar, for my house shall be called a
> house of prayer for all people (Is 56:4-7).

Toward the same time, Malachi visualizes the day when
"from the rising of the sun to its setting, a smoking incense
shall be offered to my name and a pure oblation, for great
is my name in all the places among the nations" (Mal 1:11).[8]

This trend toward universalism, however, calls for some
qualification. In fact it runs parallel to a strong nationalism,
and these two conceptions of messianism have never been
fully reconciled. The witness borne by Israel restored and
glorified, a beacon to the nations, will be instrumental to
the gathering of the redeemed. But there is a perpetual
balancing between the enlisting of the Gentiles unto the
glorification of Israel, and the missionary calling of Israel
whose appeal will be heeded by throngs of foreigners on
their way to the Temple: those of Midian and Epha, those
of Sheba with their presents of gold and frankincense,
singing praises to Yahweh (Is 60:6). Christian liturgies for
the feast of the Theophany have appropriated this passage,
and the adoration of the Christ-child by the Magi (Mt 2:11)
was regarded as the fulfilment of the messianic prophecy
of the Gentiles paying homage to the God of Israel.

The relationship between the election of the Jews and
the redemption of mankind would be clarified by the New
Testament. From the beginning of his public life, Christ made
it plain that he was the Servant, sent to execute the universal

plan of salvation. The Jews should have first option, according to the terms of the covenant with Abraham. "Salvation is of the Jews," declares Jesus (John 4:22) and, to the humble woman of Canaan who implored him for her sick daughter: "I am not sent but unto the lost sheep of the house of Israel" (Mt 15:24). But the sheep refused to hear him; he would save as many of them as would heed his voice and turn to his other sheep, "which are not of this fold. These also must I bring, and there shall be one fold and one shepherd" (John 10:16).⁹ Thus was the mystery fully revealed, and the command to the apostles justified: "Go into the whole world and preach the Gospel to every creature" (Mk 16:15), "in Jerusalem and in all Judaea, and in Samaria, and unto the uttermost parts of the world" (Acts 1:8), for it had been written of old: "Out of Zion shall go forth the Law, and the word of Yahweh from Jerusalem" (Is 2:3).

The third theme flows naturally from the second. It had become increasingly clear that God's ultimate triumph and the wholesale conversion of the Gentiles did not belong in the sphere of foreseeable events, even remotely. It was imperative that believers should aim forward and upward. Short-range, long-range predictions had been overtaken by history. Hope had been deceived repeatedly and at all levels. There had been, and there would be, so it seemed, no healing of the old wounds.¹⁰ Prophecy aimed beyond human time, and turned into eschatological visions with a strong apocalyptic overtone.

The description of the "last days" had by then become a standard feature of post-exilic literature. It depicts antithetically the victory of the redeemed (Is 65:15b-25, 66:22-23), and the punishment of the rebels (Is 63:1-6, 66:15-16, 24). The announcement of the universal conflagration and the day of judgment would be resumed in the so-called "Apocalypse of the Synoptics" (Mt ch. 24; Mk ch. 13; Lk 21:8-36), in which the theme of the destruction of Jerusalem by the Romans in A.D. 70 can be said to be a type of the calamities preceding the last day of this world.¹¹ We are dealing with prophetic visions, for the mystery of the "end" is beyond intelligibility and defies the imagination of human beings. The day and the hour were unknown to Jesus Christ (Mt 24:36, Greek text; Mk 13:32). The logion and its implications are much debated by modern scholars, but there is a fair unanimity on the part of the Fathers. St. Athanasius stated the principle: "After the Logos became man, whatever he spoke on a human mode must be ascribed to his human nature," from whence it follows that, whereas "the Logos knows the hour of the end, he ignores it as a man." The Cappadocians and St. John Chrysostom are equally blunt, but endeavour to relate the logion to the general economy of the revelation.[12] The Son, in his human nature, knows what the Father revealed to him, that he may declare it to his fellow men. We are not to be told how many seconds are left of the countdown which began at the Incarnation. But the Parousia, whenever it happens, is an ineluctable certainty.

CHAPTER XII

The Mirror of the Psalms

Clement of Alexandria, the patron of Christian humanists, tells, in the first pages of the *Protreptikos,* the legend of the singer Eunomos, who was taking part in the festival at Delphi and accompanied himself on the lyre. A string of the instrument snapped, trivial accident. A cicada, giddy from the summer heat, perched on the yoke of the lyre and, lo, as she, too, sang her note, the melody sounded so divine that Eunomos was proclaimed the victor of the games. Clement saw in this anecdote a symbol of human poetry transposed to the higher octave of the Christian revelation. Was Eunomos really singing the Pythian ode, or the purer tune meet for celebrating the Triune God? "He sings, my Eunomos, the eternal song of the new harmony, the song that bears the divine Name."[1]

The Psalms, unanimously regarded as the outstanding monument of the Semitic lyre, are tuned to the high octave. Like a mirror not made by hand, they reflect for us the face of our Christ. The Hebrew title of the Book is simply *Tehillim,* "Praises." The Hebrew noun is derived from the same root as the exclamation *Hallelû-Yah,* "Praise ye the

133

Lord!" The Greek title is ψαλμοί (Lat. *psalmi*); cf. the word ψαλτήριον, one of the instruments used for the accompaniment of the Temple choirs.

The canon of Scriptures published by the Latin Council of Trent lists the Psalter as *Psalterium Davidicum,* "Psalter of David." This ascription of authorship rests on a historical tradition, of relative value, to which the Books of Samuel bear witness. In the picture which they draw of the personality of David, as an astute leader, a man of regal courage and above all, of faith, one feature stands out: the power of his artistic gifts. As a page at the court of Saul, the mad king, he was called to play on the harp, in the hope that Saul would be delivered from the evil spirit that took hold of him (1 Sam 16:14-23). Music had always been recognized in antiquity as having supernatural virtues, either for inducing a mystical trance or for exorcizing demonic powers. The Davidic authenticity of the elegy on the death of Saul and Jonathan cannot reasonably be challenged: "Thy beauty, O Israel, is slain upon the hills. How are the mighty fallen?" (2 Sam 1:19-27). The lament over Abner has every chance of being genuine: "Should Abner die a senseless death?" (2 Sam 3:33-34). Once a king in Jerusalem, David led the procession organized for bringing the Ark of Yahweh back from the land of the Philistines. "David and all the house of Israel rejoiced before Yahweh with all their might, with songs, lyres and harps, timbrels and sistra, and with cymbals" (2 Sam 6:5). While it was reserved for Solomon to build the Temple, the Chronicler attributes the organization of the cult in the provisional sanctuary of the new capital, the assignment of Levites to the choirs and the various classes of instrumentalists, to David himself, in view of the "Great Entrance" to Zion (1 Chr 15:16-28).

The leadership of David in liturgical music may easily explain why he was credited with the authorship of nearly one half of the Psalms, according to the titles written by later editors or compilers of the entire collection. The aura surrounding the poet-king seemed a sufficient reason for regarding David as the author of all the Psalms. It is, however, impossible to ascribe all the Psalms to David, for a variety of reasons.[2] Scriptural references and quotations by New Testament authors are invariably introduced under the cover of his name, much in the same way as a type of popular hymns composed on a formula devised by St. Ambrose of Milan came to be described as "Ambrosian" hymns although it is known that Ambrose was not their author.

A critical introduction to the Book of Psalms does not fall within the scope of this essay. The following remarks will suffice for our purpose. The editors of the collection prefaced each Psalm by means of short notices which we have no reason to hold for inspired; they play a role similar to that of rubrics in a liturgical book. They vary considerably, from the standard Hebrew text generally followed by the Latin Vulgate, to the Septuagint. They indicate the literary type of each unit, whether a hymn of praise, or a psalm, or an elegy, or a song, or a prayer of supplication or thanksgiving, or a didactic poem. There is little agreement on the precise meaning of the technical terms, and not much more on the musical notations for choral execution, indicating what instruments should be used or the tune to which the words should be sung.[3] Nor should credit be given unreservedly to such notices as purport to specify the circumstances in which such or such a psalm, especially those attributed to David, was composed, for instance: Ps 3, "Of David, when he fled before his son Absalom" (cf. 2 Sam 15:3ff); Ps 34, "Of David, when he played the fool before Abimelech" (cf. 1 Sam 21; 10-15); Ps 51, "Of David, when the prophet Nathan came to him, after he had gone in to Bathsheba" (2 Sam ch. 11-12); Ps 57, "Of David, when he fled from Saul in the cave" (cf. 1 Sam 24:1ff). Clearer and more informative are the rubrics assigning such and such piece for the celebration of the sabbath, or some week or festive day. Indications of authorship, David or the leaders of the Temple choirs, Korah, Asaph, or individual cantors, may, to a certain extent, help to determine the formation of the Psalter, from the grouping of successive collections, into the actual arrangement of the Book.[4] St. Jerome did not like the division into five books, and preferred a continual listing of the Psalms.[5] Regarding the

date of composition of the single psalms, there is a bewildering variety of opinions. The commonly accepted range is
between the late tenth century B.C. (epoch of David), and
the post-exilic period, with the possibility of a few Maccabaean psalms. All these speculations are highly hypothetical
and are secondary for our purpose. A sharper focusing on
the prophetic books had been needed because of their greater
involvement in the historical process. But the goal of the
psalms is to promote an immediate relationship with God;
and, even when they reflect the concrete human predicament,
they depend less on temporal conditions. They are not only
to be read or commented in the school but to be chanted
in the church.

Even prior to the definitive codification,[6] the psalms
had given voice and expression to the worship of the Jews.
The Torah and the prophets provided the lessons, but the
Psalter was the hymnal of the Temple. Used freely at first,
it became soon regulated by rubrics assigning certain psalms
to special seasons of prayer or to festive celebrations, a
practice standardized in Late Judaism and in the majority
of Christian churches.[7] It had been the prayer book of Christ
and the apostles; it would inspire our hymnographers and
liturgists.

According to the title notices, some psalms were designated
for the Temple services on appointed dates. Most of these
rubrics occur only in the Greek version. This may indicate
either that the prototype used by the translators was different from the current Hebrew text, or it may witness to a
late organization in the second Temple. The reason for these
assignments is far from evident in many cases, and this
would suggest an arbitrary distribution of the psalms similar
to that of our *kathismata* or of the psalter of the Latin
breviaries.

The designation of certain psalms to feasts, anniversaries,
or seasonal rites, is of course more objectively related to
their contents. Thus, Psalm 114, "When Israel went forth
from Egypt," an Alleluia Psalm, is linked with the Paschal
celebration. Psalm 118, "O give thanks to the Lord," also

an Alleluia Psalm, with its refrain, "For he is good, his mercy endures forever," is a processional for the autumnal feast of *Sukkoth,* "the huts," the Feast *par excellence, hê-hag,* ἡ ἑορτή;[8] verse 22, recalling the days when the Temple was rebuilt after the Babylonian Exile, tells of "the stone which the builders rejected, and which has become the chief cornerstone." It proved prophetic and was applied to Christ by the authors of the New Testament (Mt 21:42, Acts 4:11, 1 Pet 2:6-7); Jesus had heard it being sung by the cantors, when he took part in the festal procession, holding a *lulab* of green branches (cf. verse 27). The Septuagint indicate that Psalm 29 (LXX 28), "Ascribe to Yahweh, O sons of God, ascribe to Yahweh glory and strength," was equally assigned to the celebration of *Sukkoth,* ἐξοδίου σκηνῆς— what we would call the "leave-taking" of the Feast; prayers and libations of water from Siloam had been added to the essential ritual of *Sukkoth* in the time of the Second Temple, to petition Yahweh for "rain in due season." As a matter of fact, Psalm 29 describes the first autumn rain, long-expected after the torrid summer months, often heralded by wind storm, dark clouds, thunder and lightning, and locally known as the "rain of Saint George."[9] Psalm 30 (LXX 29), both in Hebrew and in Greek, is, according to the rubric title, "A song for the Dedication of the Temple," probably the Second Temple, desecrated by the Syrians and purified by Judas Maccabee. The anniversary of this reconsecration became the great winter festival of the Jews, the *Hanukkah,* τὰ ἐγκαίνια, which a letter of Judas to the Egyptian Jewry calls the σκηνοπηγία of the month of *Kislew* (viz. November-December; 2 Mac:1-9) and Josephus, the Feast of Lights, τὰ φῶτα (*Antiquities* 12:228), for the lamps lighted each day of the feast in remembrance of the sacred fire of the First Temple; according to legend, it had been hidden by the priests in a dry well and was discovered and miraculously rekindled in the days of Nehemiah (2 Mac 1:18ff).[10] Such were the traditional melodies which Jesus heard from childhood, when his parents took him to Jerusalem "after the custom of the Feast" (Lk 2:42). Such was the poetry he breathed in, the familiar verses he learned

and spoke, as he conversed with his disciples or when he
poured his soul before the Father.

According to Deuteronomy 16:16, all male Israelites
that were of age were supposed to appear three times a year
before Yahweh: at the feast of the unleavened bread,
"Pascha"; at the feast of weeks, Pentecost";[11] and at the
feast of tents, "Sukkoth." A homogeneous sequence of short
Psalms (Ps 120-134) stands out, in relation to the pilgrim-
ages prescribed by the Law. They are known as the *shirê
hamma'aloth,* ᾠδαὶ τῶν ἀναβαθμῶν, the "songs of
degrees" (KJ), or "songs of ascents" (RSV).[12] A glance at
these may help us to enter into the human emotions and
feelings of Jesus Christ, whose travels through Palestine
followed the rhythm of the traditional feasts. Pilgrims looked
forward with eagerness to the recurrence of the holy days:
"I rejoiced when they said unto me: Let us go to the house
of Yahweh"; to "Jerusalem, whither the tribes go up, as
was decreed in Israel"; to Jerusalem, "built as a city firmly
bound together" (Ps 122). The Galilaeans caught their
first sight of the city from the hilltop of the Scopus: "Too
long were we among strangers, encamped in the tents of
Qedar," in the midst of the "haters of peace" (Ps 120).
"And now we shall lift up our eyes toward Zion, the
mountain of God, from whence comes our help" (Ps 121);
Zion, standing in the circle of hills that surround her, a
symbol of the protection of the Lord "round about his
people forever" (Ps 125). Those coming from the western
districts would remember the procession of the Ark, when
David brought it back from the country of the Philistines
and from the house of Obed-Edom in the "fields of Ya'ar,"
the hill of Qiryath Ye'arim, the "village in the woods,"
a few miles from Jerusalem (Ps 132). Soon they would
stand in awe before the Temple walls, truly divine structures,
for "except the Lord build the House, they labor in vain that
build it" (Ps 127). And they would enter into the sacred
courts, facing the House of which it is written: "My House
shall be called a house of prayer" (Is 56:7; Mt 21:12-13).
The days of the Feast would be spent in offerings at the

altar, prayers, hymns of praise and thanksgiving, and it would be like "the dew of Hermon which falls on the mountain of Zion, for there Yahweh has commanded the blessing, life for evermore" (Ps 133). Without any stretch of imagination, we may assume that the words of these pilgrim songs were in the heart and on the lips of Jesus and his disciples, when they went up to Jerusalem.

On the eve of the Passion (Mt 26:30), Jesus and his company sang the hymns of praise, as prescribed for the Paschal celebration, namely the so-called Egyptian Hallel (Ps 113-118), and the Great Hallel (Ps 135-136), the latter psalm being a solemn litany of thanksgiving for the marvels of the Creation and the divine guidance over the years. A third Hallel, composed of Psalms 146-150 (cf. Dan 3:51-90), was part of the customary morning prayers. It became part of the *Laudes* of the Latin liturgies, and of the αἶνοι (*Khvalitnyi*) of the Byzantine Office, prior to the Great Doxology.

Besides the popular songs and the solemn hymns of praise and thanksgiving or the didactic poems, the latter being often rhapsodies of earlier Biblical texts, the psalms sung in the Temple with accompaniment of strings, the *mizmôrim*, bear witness to the ways of Hebrew piety through the ages. Our Lord had learned them as a child, he prayed in their words and sang them in the Temple. Condemned by the leaders of his nation, abandoned by his friends, hanging from the cross, he cried with a loud voice the cry of the anonymous martyr of Psalm 22: "My God, my God, why hast thou forsaken me?" So completely had he involved himself in the common predicament of the human race that, in retrospect, the Evangelists would regard the Psalm as having a prophetic value. They remembered the lament of the unknown sufferer as they had remembered the poems of the Servant in the Book of Isaiah: "I am a worm, and not a man." The passers-by deride me, "they grin at me with their lips and wag their heads: He trusted in Yahweh, let Yahweh deliver him and rescue him, since he is his friend!. . . . They have pierced my hands and my feet . . . they divide my garments among them, and for my raiment they cast lots" (Ps 22:6-8, 16-18; cf. Mt 27:43, 35; John 19:24). Or Psalm 69:8-9, 19-21: "I am become a stranger unto my brethren, an alien to my mother's sons, for the zeal of thy house has consumed me. . . . Thou knowest my reproach, my shame and my dishonor. My enemies are all before thine eyes. . . . I looked for pity, but there was none, for a comforter, but I found none. They gave me gall for my meat, and in my thirst, they gave me vinegar to drink" (cf. John 19:29; Mt 27:34, 48).

As prayers, the psalms arise from an acute feeling of despondency: man sees himself surrounded by myriads of adversaries and national enemies. In days of alarm or disaster, the people calls upon the God of the covenant and reminds him of his promise: "Why do the heathen rage and peoples plot in vain? The kings of the earth and the princes conspire against Yahweh and against his anointed," to whom he had said: "Thou art my son; today have I begotten thee" (Ps 2:1-2, 7; cf. Acts 13-33).

The pious Jew prayed to be delivered from his personal enemies: from his own sins, of which God alone could absolve him. This affect of repentance is ubiquitous in the Book of Psalms.[13] Most characteristic is Psalm 51, the *Miserere,* abundantly used by eastern and western liturgies.

God is called upon to protect the faithful against open and hidden dangers, against perils lurking in the dark. Thus the evening psalm: "He that dwells in the shelter of the Most High shall abide under the shadow of the Almighty. . . . Thou shalt not fear the terror by night nor the arrow that flies by day, nor the pestilence that stalks in darkness, nor the destruction that wastes at noon. A thousand shall fall at thy side, ten thousand at thy right hand, but nought shall come nigh thee. For he gives his angels charge over thee, to keep thee in all thy ways. On their hands shall they bear thee, lest thou dash thy foot against some stone" (Ps 91, passim). The supreme irony is that the devil chose precisely these last two verses, that he might tempt Jesus, whom he had made to stand precariously on the pinnacle of the Temple (Mt 4:5-6).

The dominant affect is an unwavering trust in God, and it was fitting that the Church would draw from psalms of entreaty, a group relatively distinct in the Psalter, the central motive of the service of Vespers: "Lord, I cry unto thee, hear me, O God," ἐκέκραξα Κύριε, together with the appropriate *stikhera*.[14]

The believer shall pray for deliverance from persecutors, a theme frequently recurring in the Psalter. We quote again selected verses from Psalm 69, cries for help and curses on those who afflict the just:

> Save me, O God, for the waters rose up to my soul! I sink in deep mire, where I have no footing. . . . They that hurt me without cause . . . are more than the hairs of my head. Mighty are those who seek to destroy me, those who accuse me calumniously: What I did not steal, am I then to give it back? . . . It is for thy sake that I bear reproach, that shame covers my face. . . . I am the talk of those who sit at the gate and the song of the drunkards. . . . O God, in the multitude of thy mercies answer me, in the truth of thy salvation. Let the table of my oppressors be a snare unto them, and their sacred meals a trap![15] Let their eyes be darkened, that they see no more, and make their loins fail forever! . . . Let their encampment be desolate and their tents empty! . . . Let them be blotted out of the book of the living, that they not be counted with the righteous!

All along the Book of Psalms, we hear the groans of the humble, the poor, the downtrodden, of defenseless widows and orphans, derided, cheated, oppressed by prosperous rascals, greedy bullies and rotten judges. The victims are the same as those in whose favor the eighth-century prophets lifted their voices, and they can appeal but to God for redress, and perhaps vengeance, their ardent supplication alternating with angry curses and fiery imprecations. Their cries would be heard. We are assured that they did not call in vain upon the Messiah. The Beatitudes (Mt 5:1-12, Lk 6:20-23) echo the Psalms and the Prophets. The poor and the meek shall inherit the earth (cf. Ps 37:11). Those who mourn shall be comforted; having sown in tears, they shall reap in joy (Ps 126:6). Those who hunger after righteousness shall be filled (Is 51:7). The merciful shall obtain mercy, "for God has shown thee, O man, what is good: to do justly and to love mercy" (Mic 6:8). The pure in heart shall see God, as Moses saw him on his holy mountain (cf. Ps 24:3-4). The peacemakers shall be called sons of God (cf. 82:6). Those who are persecuted for righteousness' sake, who are reviled and accused falsely, like the poor man of Psalm 69, great is their reward in heaven!

The last enemy to be overcome is death. It was not among the creatures which God pronounced good; it was the fatal sanction of Adam's disobedience. Man had his destiny in his hands: it was possible that he would not die; had he met the test of obedience successfully, he would have become positively immortal and could not be overcome by death. Once a sinner, alienated from God, he could not possibly *not* die. God is master over life and death. He is "he that kills and makes live" (Deut 32:39). But once death has struck, is it in his power to recall to life those who are in the tomb? And since the issues of life and death are linked with the economy of God's judgments, would it be that justice is denied to those whom death has overcome, before the wrong that was made to them is corrected? The Psalmist has no certain answer to those questions.

On the one hand, the Jews shared with the other peoples of the Near and Middle East the common vision of the dead lying in the grave, and whose decaying remains retain only a token identity. Can their shadow-like continuation of existence in the *shé'ol,* the *'abaddon,*[16] be called immortality? The dead are excluded from every communication with the living and with the Living God; "the slain that lie in the grave, whom thou rememberest no more, they are cut off from thy hand . . . in the lowest pit, in darkness, in the deeps. . . . For the dead dost thou work wonders? Do the shadows rise up and praise thee? Is thy lovingkindness declared in the grave, thy faithfulness in *'abaddon?*" (Ps 88:5-6, 10-11; see also Ps 6:5; 115:17-18).

On the other hand, even if we exclude such texts as Psalm 30:3, where deliverance from *shé'ol* is a metaphor for God's help in a desperate situation, or 68:20, which refers to the nation being rescued from disaster, some psalms insinuate without positively affirming that it is not beyond God's power to restore the dead to life. The link between the prospect of immortality or resurrection and the demands of justice is here again dominant. It seemed indecent that a righteous God would abandon in death forever him who had chosen God as his part of inheritance, thus Psalm 16:10: "Thou shalt not let me go down to *shē'ol*, nor wilt thou let thy devoted one see the pit" or, according to the versions and the earliest Christian tradition (Acts 2:27 and 13:35), "see corruption (διαφθοράν)." It should be noted that Judaism, which shared the latter exegesis, had admitted the messianism of Psalm 16, and that St. Paul, preaching in the synagogue at Antioch of Pisidia, could proclaim that Jesus was the Messiah "whom God raised from the dead, that he would not see corruption" (Acts 13:35).

The final verse of Psalm 17—the Psalm of the third hour—expresses even a positive hope: "As for me, I shall behold thy face in righteousness, and when I wake up, I will be satisfied with thy form, *temûnathéka*," a difficult word, supposing a real perception, not an imaginary vision; (cf. Num 12:8). A minimizing exegesis would understand "waking up" (verse 15) as from natural sleep; but what is at stake is the liberation of the Psalmist from the relentless intrigues of his enemies, and this calls for something more than the feeling of elation following a night's rest. It demands redress, and that death not be allowed to thwart the satisfaction of divine justice. This is what the versions have understood, LXX: "I shall be satisfied with beholding thy Glory, ἐν τῷ ὀφθῆναι δόξα σου," Vulg.: "when thy Glory shall appear, *cum apparuerit gloria tua.*"

Psalm 49 develops the same theme by means of an antithesis between insolent rich and the victims of their pride and luxury, Yahweh's poor. The evil rich will be driven by death into *shē'ol*, where his figure shall decay, while "God will ransom my soul and grab me from Hades," that I may be ultimately vindicated (verse 15).

The light which the Psalms throw on human destiny is but a glimmer in the dark. Not until Christ arises from the tomb, having trampled death by death, will men walk in the light of the noonday. Not until God's sons and daughters, following in the footsteps of their master, have passed through the portal of death, shall they enter with full knowledge into the blessedness of Trinitarian life, forever to be shared.

CHAPTER XIII

The Books
of Divine Wisdom

In the preceding chapters, we have generally followed the traditional order of the books in the Hebrew Bible: the Law, the Prophets, and the *Ketûbim,* that is, "the 'other' Scriptures," plus the books of the Alexandrian canon.[1] The Book of Psalms had to be treated separately, due to its exceptional importance in the prayer life of the Hebrew nation and of the Christian Church, although it is recensed by the Jews among the *Ketûbim.* The present chapter, therefore, will deal with the following: the Book of Job (early fifth century B.C.), a debate between Job and his friends on the problem of human suffering, and the Wisdom Books strictly speaking, namely: the Book of Proverbs, Παροιμίαι (fifth century B.C.), being a collection of sentences attributed to Solomon and other sages; Qohéleth, or Ecclesiastes (third century B.C.), also ascribed to Solomon, "the words of Qohéleth, son of David. . . . I, Qohéleth, was king in Jerusalem"; it is a plea for moderation by a sage professing detachment from all sorts of intransigeance or pedantry; the apocryphal Wisdom of Solomon, Σοφία Σολομῶνος, not extant in the Hebrew Bible, written in Greek by an unknown Hellenistic Jew in the course of the first century B.C.; and the Wisdom of Jesus, son of Sirach, Σοφία Σειράχ, Ecclesiasticus, also deuterocanonical; it seems to have been composed in Hebrew by a scribe in the first half of the second century B.C.; fragments of a Hebrew text, often at variance with the Greek, were discovered in 1896-1900.

Such classifications have only a limited regard to chronology or history. However it is possible to distinguish three "movements" in the development of revelation as a whole, for it is anything but static. The first movement corresponds to dogmatic statements on God the creator and guardian of laws governing the universal order. The second is that of the covenant-relationship of Yahweh with the Fathers, codified in the Books of Moses and freed from legalistic mechanization by the latter prophets. The third, after the collapse of the kingdoms, opens broad eschatological prospects and an extension of the covenant to all mankind.

The differences between these three movements should not be exaggerated.[2] There are not three Old Testament religions having little in common except for the fact that they have been professed by successive generations of the same people. Nor should one try to explain them as three phases superseding one another in the evolutionary process. We would rather think in terms of providential transpositions of a unique revelational theme historically conditioned. One important factor in the last movement is the pervasiveness of Hellenistic culture in post-exilic Judaism, both in Palestine and in the Diaspora. This dictates our task in the present chapter: revisiting, from the vantage point of late Jewish and Alexandrian literature, some of the capital themes of Old Testament economy.[3]

The overall ascription of the Book of Proverbs to Solomon is very similar to that of the Psalms to David (cf. above ch. 12). The annalists have recorded Solomon's proverbial wisdom, "greater than the wisdom of the *Benê Qédem,* the 'Sons of the East,' and all the wisdom of Egypt"; the "three thousand maxims he composed"; his knowledge of plants, "from the cedar of Lebanon to the hyssop," and of "the beasts, fowl, creeping things, and fish" (1 Ki 5:29-34); his shrewdness in the courtroom (1 Ki 3:16-28); his contest with the Queen of Sheba at solving riddles (1 Ki 10:1-13). Just as the Psalms composed by the Levites and the cantors of the Temple were edited with those which David had composed or which were attributed to him as the creator of the Temple hymnal, miscellaneous aphorisms attributed to Solomon (Prov 10:16) were gathered together with maxims of the royal scribes, a hierarchy of government officials instituted on the model of the Pharaonic bureaucracy,[4] with sayings of the Arab sages Agur and Lemuel (Prov 30:1 and 31:1), or with sentences collected by the scribes of Hezekiah, king of Judah, who credited them to Solomon as the father of gnomic literature among the Hebrews (Prov 25:1).

The wisdom of the scribes is rather short-winded. It consists of advices of prudence and moderation from a well-meaning father to his son, rules of ethical behavior and courtesy, and a harvest of popular sayings, often trite, occasionally humorous, but seldom lacking the salt and the causticity of the Sumero-Akkadian proverbs. Some show forth the artificiality of such literary exercises as the acrostic[5] to the praise of the perfect wife (Prov 31:10-31), or the numerical proverbs, for instance: "Three things escape me, and four I cannot know: the path of the eagle in the sky, of the serpent on a rock, of a ship on the high sea, or of a man in a maiden" (Prov 30:18-19).[6]

The editors of the Jerusalem Bible, in their introductory notice to the Book of Proverbs, write that the dominant note in the maxims it contains is that of "a profane wisdom, disconcerting to the Christian reader." However, among the uninspiring sermons of father to son on the desirability of wisdom,[7] the tune rises occasionally to a praise of Divine Wisdom at work in creation and in the world of men, transcending the prudential considerations of the first seven chapters. Wisdom, now personified as a divine hypostasis, pronounces her own panegyric, for she alone is equal to that object: "When there were no depths, I was begotten, when there were no fountains gushing forth with water, before the mountains were firmly rooted, earlier than the hills was I begotten. ... I was at his side as master-builder, making his delight day by day, playing before him always, playing on the surface of the earth, and my delights are with the sons of men" (Prov 8:24-25, 30-31).

On the very eve of the Incarnation, the identity of Wisdom as Logos and divine energy,[8] was nigh revealed: "Wisdom, mobile above all motion, penetrating and pervading all things thanks to her purity, for she is a breathing of the power of God, a diffusion of the glory of the Almighty, into her nothing defiled may gain entrance. She is a reflection of Light eternal, a spotless mirror of God's activity and an icon of his goodness . . . reaching from one end of the world to the other, and governing all things with beneficence" (Wis 7:24-26 and 8:1).

Having recorded the days of Eden, the Bible outlines an ascension from the elementary wisdom of fallen man, self-conscious, cautious and clever, to an ethical concern for his fellow men, and finally to a participation in the God-given splendor that visits him—a mere shadow in the night— through the bright radiance that plays over him.[9] The revelation of Divine Wisdom thus leads in a straight line to the Prologue of the Fourth Gospel, the next step being the humanization of the Logos, unto the mystery of the deification of man, which will be revealed on the last day.

From the eighth century B.C. onward, the seemingly unjust suffering of innocents and the apparent impunity of perpetrators of crimes against the common good had been a scandal to both prophets and psalmists. The problem, which the national disaster and the circumstances of the Exile and the post-exilic resettlement had rendered more acute, was scrutinized but not solved—theological problems seldom are—by the authors of the *Ketûbim* and of the books of the Greek canon of Scriptures. A literature of protest was developed by academic disputers, and it is this protest that we would examine now. The Law had emphasized the collective responsibility of the covenanted people before God. It had its roots in tribal customs, and it formed the dynamic center of moral and social justice. In a context of cultic values, namely the prohibition of idolatry, the Law had stated that sin, inasmuch as it involved the responsibility of the entire nation, would be visited not only on the individual culprit, but on his descendants, "for I, the Lord, am a jealous God, visiting the iniquity of the fathers upon the children unto the third and fourth generation of them that hate me, and showing mercy unto thousands of them that love me and keep my commandments" (Ex 20:5-6, Deut 5:9-10). The announcement of the sanction was meant as a deterrent and its counterpart as an incentive unto obedience. But it could be misinterpreted, and in fact it was, for it became often a cheap pretext for shrugging off one's personal responsibility without bothering too much about religious, moral or social obligations. It was easy to repeat, in times of trouble, the popular saying: "The fathers have eaten sour grapes, and the children's teeth are on edge." So tenacious was the prejudice, that we hear the disciples of Jesus, who had met a man born blind, ask of the Master: "Rabbi, who did sin, this man, or his parents?" (John 9:2). The prophets hated the old proverb and countered with the unconditional statement that "every one shall be stricken for his own iniquity" (Jer 31:29-30, Ezek 18:2-4). Nobody would disagree with the principle, but daily experience had shown too many instances of the wicked being exalted and the pious gratuitously afflicted; we have heard the bitter complaints of the victims in the Psalms, and the fiery denunciation of all forms of injustice by the prophets.

The problem of human suffering is discussed at length in the Book of Job. No lengthy introduction is needed here; the story is well-known. The action takes place somewhere in Arabia. Job is not a Jew, but one of the *Benê Qêdem,* issued of Abraham by his concubines, living in a patriarchal setup. Obviously, the redactor tries to state the problem in universal terms, rather than within the restricted framework of the Mosaic institution. Satan has challenged God to submit Job's virtue to the acid test of suffering. The righteous man is stricken successively in his possessions, his children, his own flesh, and sits, abandoned by his kin, covered with ulcers, having for companions the stray dogs that haunt the town dump. A trio of his "friends" come and discuss his case with him, urging him to scan his life in order to discover what may have been the cause of his affliction. The self-appointed inquisitors find actually nothing which would warrant the terrible punishment to which he is submitted, but there must have been something. Now a young theologian, garrulous and knowing everything better, joins our worthies and recites his lesson. It is all very simple: "You have sinned, therefore you must suffer punishment. You suffer, then you have certainly sinned, some place, some time!" Job cannot but protest of his innocence and appeal to the just judgment of God, who finally exonerates him and restores him in his earlier prosperity, without revealing the transcendent secret of his Providence.

The problem is humanly insoluble, and this explains the pessimism of a Qohéleth, who has given up trying to lift would it be only a corner of the veil. It is all labor lost: "I have set my heart to seek and to explore through wisdom everything that happens under the sky, a sore business which God gave to the sons of Adam to busy themselves with. I have considered whatever is being done under the sun, and behold, all is vanity and pursuit of wind" (Eccle 1:12-14). Fate, luck, the wheel of fortune, are meaningless words; the regular occurrence of natural events, the alternance of joy and grief in a human life can be described, they cannot be explained. The mystery of life and death are in God's hand, as are justice and the balance of the cosmos. We must leave their disposition to God, and we may listen to the sobering advice of another sage: "Seek not what is to much for your grasp, and probe not into that which is above your power" (Eccli 3:22).

The Jews had been led to wonder, since justice on this earth seems to be thwarted repeatedly, whether the solution of the problem of a just retribution is not rather to be sought after this life? But where, how, and when? Qohéleth had unceremoniously dismissed the whole idea: "Who knows whether the spirit of the sons of Adam goes upward, whether the spirit of the beasts goes down to the earth?" (Eccle 3:21). Could the dead be raised to a new life, in order that justice, which seems to have been denied to them, might be fulfilled, and the sinner convicted and punished? It had not been revealed unto the fathers, nor announced by the prophets, nor could anyone come up from the grave and instruct the living.[10] One thing only was certain: Yahweh, the author of life, has an equal power over death, which he did not make. Death will not reign forever. As a harbinger of the messianic triumph, "when Death will be swallowed in victory" (Is 25:8), when Yahweh will put flesh and sinews on "very many and very dry bones and breathe on them the breath of life" (Ezek 37:1-14), several humans who had slept in death were reported to have been miraculously raised up from the dead: the son of the widow of Zarephath (1 Ki 17:17-22), the son of the Shunamite (2 Ki 4:32-37).[11] These anecdotes, however, suppose that life was not definitively restored; these men would again have to die!

The restoration of life toward which the Hebrews were looking must be understood as a resurrection of some sort, in conformity with their anthropological ideas. They thought of man primarily as a person, *néphesh,* a material aggregate: the lump of clay out of which Adam had been formed, animated by the *rûah,* which is in fact the breath of life which Yahweh had breathed into it.[12] A partial survival, *a fortiori* the problematic continuation of existence in the *shé'ol,* could not possibly meet the requirements for a satisfaction of justice. Job expresses this in a passionate cry, which has been appropriately used by the Latin liturgists for the vigil of the dead: "I know that my redeemer lives[13] and that he will stand last on the earth. From behind my skin I shall stand, in my own flesh I will see Eloah,[14] whom I shall see myself, whom my eyes shall behold, I, and not another" (Job 19:25). On the part of Job, this was a cry of faith and hope, not a dogmatic statement. Many, even among the pious, did not dare to look that far.

A few centuries later, the author of the Books of the

Maccabees, reflecting on the sacrifice which Judas offered for those who had fallen in battle against the Syrians, reminded his contemporaries that this had been a most religious deed, "for if he were not expecting that those who had fallen would rise again, it would have been superfluous and foolish to pray for the dead" (2 Mac 12:43-44). This striving toward the belief in the resurrection of the dead, diversely expressed in the intertestamentary period, especially among the Pharisees and the sectarians, is in opposition to the radical negations of the Sadducees, but also in contrast with the developing influence of Hellenistic philosophy on late Jewish thought.

The author of the Book of Wisdom, reviewing the themes of death and moral retribution, whose mutual connection the psalmists, Job and a few others had sensed as by instinct but had been unable to express clearly, starts from different premises. He had no intention of disavowing his predecessors, whose influence, although not leading, can be sporadically traced in his writing. The problem remained much the same, but with a distinct eschatological orientation; the Pseudo-Solomon worked within the categories of a modified Platonism. Man was seen as a being composed of flesh and spirit, two elements accidentally united and in tension with each other. The former element is subject to alteration, decay and corruption. The latter, of itself, is impassible, incorruptible, imperishable. The drama of man is that the spirit, on account of its temporary incarnation, is captive of the body, enslaved to conditions of time and space, involved in all sorts of miseries, illusions, and deviations from the ideal norm fixed by God, "for the corruptible body weighs down the soul, and its camping on earth oppresses the mind rich in thoughts" (Wis 9:15). Death, therefore, is a liberation more than a punishment. Sin shall cease; justice, vindicated, shall reign over the righteous and the wise; the goal is positive immortality, but only for the good. Death and decay is the lot of the wicked, and their condition in *shĕ'ol* is a prospect more repugnant to nature than, for the Greek, the semi-permanence of the personality and semi-consciousness of the dead in the house of Hadès. The Sage, therefore, outlines, in a chain of syllogisms, the program of a journey to eternity: "The beginning of wisdom is a desire for instruction. The care of instruction is unto love. To love is to keep the laws of Wisdom. Keeping her laws is an assurance of immortality. Immortality makes one to be near God. . . . Therefore the desire of wisdom leads to the kingdom. . . . Seek ye, then, wisdom, that you may reign forever" (Wis 6:17-21).

It would be totally inappropriate to pitch the embryonic idea of resurrection, met sporadically in Hebrew literature, against the elaborate but unilateral doctrine of immortality of the Book of Wisdom.[15] They stand in contrast, not in contradiction. They are the material for a synthesis, which it is not given to mortals to achieve, and which only the Resurrection of Christ makes true. The resurrection of the dead was nonsense to the hearers of St. Paul on Mars Hill, who were curious to hear what he had to say concerning the immortality of the soul. Yet the Hebrews were right, when they looked forward to "the resurrection on the last day." This would be a resurrection of the whole man and of all men, since the whole man, not his spirit alone, had played, toiled, loved, hated, sinned, and suffered in his earthly life. And the immortality of the human soul, breathed by God in a mortal clay, justifies the expectation of all the saints in all the ages, of the Fathers of the Old Law, who have been received in Abraham's bosom, of all who shall fall asleep before the final judgment and the final triumph.

The Church unanimously acknowledged, after only a few decades of her life, the coexistence of the belief in the resurrection and that of the immortality of the soul, assuming the fact of an intermediary status of the dead, whose identity is maintained, without the somatic conditioning of the human person. It is expressed metaphorically in the prayers for the dead, that it please God "to give rest to the souls of his departed servants in a place of brightness, a place of verdure, a place of repose, from which all sickness and sorrow have fled away." There can, of course, be no conclusive argument for what remains an assumption in faith on the part of the "wayfarers." It is only from beyond death and

resurrection that full evidence will be perceived by humans.
For the time being, two words from the Gospel tell all that
needs to be told concerning resurrection and eternal life.
The first one is the word of Martha, sister of Lazarus:
"I know that he shall rise again at the resurrection on the
last day" (John 11:24). The second is the word of Jesus,
answering from the cross to the prayer of Dysmas: "Today
thou shalt be with me in Paradise" (Lk 23-43).

Concluding Postscript

With each step of our journey through the Bible, we have tried to discern the face of Christ amidst the shadows of the past, in figure, in type, in prophecy, following in the steps trodden by the Fathers of the Church. We read frequently in the footnotes of our English Bibles such sentences as: "Christian tradition has understood this passage in such or such a way," or "This is what the Fathers have read back into this saying of the Old Testament." I have used these formulae myself although, frankly, I do not like them, for they may give the impression of some arbitrary interpretation, or gratuitous assumption, or some artificial exercise in allegorism. This need not be. The tradition we are allegedly reading back into the Old Testament was there in the making, when anonymous editors or compilers, Ezra perhaps, gathered together the records of divine revelation and made them the Books of Scriptures which the Church puts in our hands as the source of our doctrine and our worship.

A fact, insignificant in appearance, is indicative of the close ties of the liturgy with the general economy of the revelation: in several uncial manuscripts of the Septuagint, the text of the Scriptures according to the Greek canon is followed by a collection of liturgical ᾠδαί, Lat. *cantica,* from the various books of the Old and the New Testaments, and by the Great Doxology. These odes unfold before us the entire mystery of God's economy of salvation; they have been chosen as the basic theme of our Byzantine canons, or distributed among the psalms of *Laudes* in various Latin liturgies and in the Mozarabic breviary. They recapitulate the highlights of our Bible reading and bring our study to its proper conclusion.

In the Byzantine liturgies, the first ode is the triumphal hymn of Moses and the *Benê Israel* after their miraculous escape from Egypt (Ex 15:1-19), when Yahweh opened for them a path through the waters of the sea and led them through the wilderness to the streams of the Jordan. Some day these would be sanctified by the baptism of Christ, and the Church rejoices, "that through water and the Spirit sons have been born to her," and when the Israelites were about to enter the Promised Land, Moses again sang to the Rock from which he had drawn water in the desert (Deut 32:1-43): "Now, they all drank from that spiritual Rock, and the Rock was Christ" (1 Cor 10:4).

The third ode is the hymn of thanksgiving which Hannah, the mother of Samuel, intoned on the day when "she lent him to the Lord," in the sanctuary at Shiloh (1 Sam 2:1-10), as Mary would do when she presented the infant Jesus in the Temple of Jerusalem.

The psalm of Habakkuk (3:1-19) provides the theme for the fourth ode of the canon. It attains to cosmic amplitude: "Eloah comes from Teman, the Holy One from Mount Paran. . . . Before him goes forth pestilence, a fiery plague before his feet. The everlasting mountains are scattered, the eternal heights fall down. . . . Thou goest forth to save thy people, to save thy Messiah. . . . I hear, and my belly shudders, my lips quiver at the voice. . . . Yet will I rejoice in the Lord, exult in the God of my salvation." The Latin Vulgate has rendered these last words by: *in Deo Jesu meo,* "in God my *Iesu,*" no translation indeed, but a daring play on the etymology of the name: Jesus, cf. *yésha,* salvation (Mt 1:21).

The fifth ode is taken from Isaiah 26:9-20, a song of hope: "For the dead shall live, their bodies shall rise. O dwellers in the dust, awake and shout for joy, for thy dew is a dew of light, and on the land of shadow thou wilt make it fall." The sixth ode is a further announcement of the resurrection; it tells the story of Jonah, who was rendered to light after three days in the belly of the fish, a sign, nay *the* sign to an incredulous generation, and none other but this sign would be given to them (Mt 12:40), seeing that Jesus would submit freely to the monstrous power of death, and the third day rise victorious from the tomb.

The hymn of deliverance of the three young Hebrews in the furnace of fire, theme of the seventh and the eighth odes, (Dan 3:26-45 and 52-88), brings to a close the series of Old Testament figures. It is the answer of a redeemed mankind to the call heard from the midst of the burning bush, and it voices the unceasing praise of the Church, amidst the fires of sin.

We stand now on the threshold of the Gospel. It behooved Zacharias, a priest of the order of Aaron, to give thanks for the birth of his son, who would prepare the ways of the Savior, the Eternal Priest after the order of Melchizedek (Lk 1:68-79), as it would belong to Mary, the Theotokos and Mother of Light, to magnify the Lord in accents echoing the canticle of Hannah (Lk 1:46-55). And when the day came for the Theotokos to bring her son to the Temple, two prophetic voices were heard: the voice of Simeon, who came by the Spirit into the Temple, took the child in his arms and blessed God, for he saw "Him who was set for the fall and rising again of many in Israel"; and the voice of Ann the prophetess, "who spake of Him to all of them that looked for redemption in Jerusalem" (Lk 2:27-32).

The long vigil is ended. The day has dawned. Types, figures, and prophecies have ceased. The old order has passed away. Immanuel was born, died, and rose from the dead. We have entered the new aeon.

Saint Damien de Brandon (Québec), the sixth day of August 1974, in the Feast of the Holy Transfiguration of Our Lord God and Saviour Jesus Christ.

Notes

CHAPTER I

[1]*In festo S. Caeciliae, ad vesperas (Breviarium S. Ord. Praed.)*

[2]*Concio 3 de Lazaro,* PG 48:992.

[3]*Hom. 35 de Genesi,* PG 53:323.

[4]*Epist.* 128, PL 22:1098.

[5]*Epist.* 79, PL 22:730 f.

[6]*Russian Theology, 1920-1965: A Bibliographical Survey* (Richmond, Va., 1969).

[7]It should be remembered that we know Marcion only through the quotations and reports of his adversaries. For a summary of his teachings, see H. Lietzmann, *A History of the Early Church* (New York, 1953) pp. 249-263.

[8]Authoritative presentation of the dualistic heresy in Armenia and Eastern Europe, Nina G. Garsoian, *The Paulician Heresy* (The Hague and Paris, 1967). Summary information on the heretical groups in mediaeval Europe, Stephen Runciman, *The Medieval Manichee* (Cambridge, 1947).

[9]Athanasius, *Adv. Arianos* 2:59, PG 26:273.

[10]*Paed.* 1:6, PG 8:280. Origen imagined a paedagogical device by means of which Christ, by asking rhetorical questions, would in fact teach the doctors, while observing the modesty which befits a twelve-year-old, *Hom. 19 in Lucam,* PG 8:280.

[11]H. Denzinger, *Enchiridion symbolorum,* n° 148.

[12]*In Titum* 2:9, PL 26:630.

[13]*Praefatio in Job.*

[14]*Adv. Rufin.* 3:6, PL 23:483.

[15]We fervently hope that the updating experiments of the churches in the Roman communion will not radically depart from the basic principles and the traditional patterns of their liturgies, which generally antedate the rupture between East and West.

CHAPTER II

[1]Cf. the so-called Rule of St. Augustine: *Hoc versetur in corde, quod profertur in ore,* "Let that dwell in your heart, which your mouth utters." *Epist.* 211, PL 33:960.

[2]*Confessiones* 9:6.

[3]*In Ezek. Hom.* 7, PL 76:846.

[4]Cf. G. J. Renier, *History, Its Purpose and Method* (London, 1950) p. 49.

[5]Morton White, *Foundations of Historical Knowledge* (New York, 1965) p. 208 f.

[6]This book, published in 1903, was re-edited with an updating preface by the late Père de Vaux, Paris, 1966.

[7]I am thinking here of the late Fr. Lagrange, who regretted that "the imperious necessity of the times had confined him and his early collaborators in the narrow field of critical exegesis." Cf. Henri de Lubac, S. J., *L'Ecriture dans la Tradition* (Paris, 1966) p. 291. The quotation is from a letter of the late Fr. Hugues Vincent to Mgr. de Solages.

[8]The contemporary revival of patristic studies in the Roman Church met at first with mistrust in Vatican circles, as some theologians were concerned lest it might be interpreted as a downgrading of the dogmatic apparatus of Roman theology and the official doctrine of Thomas Aquinas.

[9]The inspiration (θεοπνευστία) of the Scriptures guarantees proportionally the authority of the versions used in the Church, as well as of the original texts in the Hebrew and the Alexandrian canon. The inspiration of the LXX recently has been debated by Roman theologians. As a matter of fact, the Latin Church has always regarded the LXX as an "authentic version" but has made no pronouncement regarding its inspiration. Cf. P. Benoit, "La Septante est-elle inspirée?" in *Vom Wort des Lebens* (Max Meinertz' Festschrift; Muenster i. W., 1951).

[10]*Adv. haer.* 3:21-23, PG 7:954-960, passim.

CHAPTER III

[1]Cf. H. de Lubac, *L'Ecriture dans la Tradition* (Paris, 1966) p. 133.

[2]Cf. the suggestive name of the *Via degli formatori* in Rome, where commercial artists and artisans have their workshops.

[3]A saying which belongs, like many others, in the *agrapha* of the professor, faithfully preserved in the memory of his Princeton neighbors and friends.

[4]Inasmuch as we can speak of a system; at any rate it is not a closed system. Teilhard's theological works consist almost entirely of short essays, often mimeographed for private distribution among his friends. For an overall presentation and a concentrated bibliography, see F. Mooney, S. J., *Teilhard de Chardin and the Mystery of Christ* (New York, 1966). On the Orthodox side, Teilhard's work has attracted the attention of another

scientist specialized in biological and genetic research, Professor Theodosius Dobzhansky, who insists on the unpredictability of evolution; he infers from this that there must be a divine meaning to the mysterious development of living species.

[5]On form criticism, its use and abuse, see V. Kesich, *The Gospel Image of Christ* (Crestwood, N. Y., 1972) p. 14 ff.

[6]The Greek conjunctions used in these locutions introduce nuances of meaning foreign to Hebrew or Aramaic, which would have used such vague particles as *asher, shé, ki;* these merely indicate the fact of a connection between several propositions, the exact nature of this connection being determined by the context. Passages referring to individuals or groups deliberately blinded by God, "that seeing they may not see," represent an extreme case, which needs not be discussed here.

[7]H. de Lubac, *op. cit.,* p. 21.

[8]*De arca Noe morali* 2:8, PL 176:642.

[9]*De doctrina christiana* 3, PL 34:80.

[10]Cf. H. de Lubac, *op. cit.,* p. 24. In modern parlance, allegory has become synonymous with an arbitrary figure of speech, loosely connected, or not connected at all, with the objective reality directly expressed by a literal statement.

[11]This mnemotechnic jingle dates from the late thirteenth century. On the methods of Biblical scholarship in the Western Church during the Middle Ages, see Beryl Smalley, *The Study of the Bible in the Middle Ages* (Oxford, 1941).

[12]Thus Aquinas: "The literal sense is not the figure itself, but that which is expressed by means of the figure," *Summa Theologiae, Prima Pars,* qu. 1, art. 10, ad 3m.

[13]*Summa Theologiae, Prima Pars,* qu. 1, art. 10. The realism of Aquinas in formulating these principles is akin to the Dionysian conception of the hierarchic structure of the real, in contrast with Augustine's world of rhetorical symbols.

[14]*Comment. in Psalmos, praef.,* PG 80:860.

[15]*De poenitentia hom.* 6, PG 49:320.

[16]H. de Lubac, *op. cit.,* p. 19.

CHAPTER IV

[1]"Sorted out." Hebrew *habdîl,* to separate, to distinguish; LXX: δια-χωρίζω. Cf. the *opus distinctionis* of the Latin commentators.

[2]Hebrew *sabâ,* pl. *sebâoth;* hence God's traditional title, "Lord of the armies."

[3]Without the article in the Hebrew text of verse 26; LXX: ἄνθρωπον.

[4]On the sources of the Pentateuch, see Arthur Weiser, *The Old Testament: Its Formation and Development* (New York, 1961; reprinted last in 1968) pp. 69-99.

[5]Ugarit is the ancient name of the site, the exploration of which began in 1929 and has continued ever since.

[6]From the Assyrian text. A more literary rendering of the entire epic is found in James B. Pritchard, *Ancient Near Eastern Texts* (Princeton, 1950) p. 60 ff.

[7]The advance of the shoreline toward the southeast, relative to the presumed shoreline in the Neo-Babylonian period, is of approximately 160 miles.

[8]Cf. the Chaldaean cosmogony: "No brick mould had been made yet, no house built, no town founded."

[9]Texts in translation, with an introduction by Cyrus H. Gordon, *Ugaritic Literature* (Rome, 1949).

[10]David Neiman, "The Polemic Language of the Genesis Cosmology," in *The Heritage of the Early Church* (Festschrift Georges Florovsky; Rome, 1973) pp. 47-63.

[11]The Hebrew words have passed unchanged into the French locution *tohubohu = vacarme,* radical disorder.

[12]The "tumultuous Tiâmat," a personification of the sea, *tamtu.* Cf. the Hebrew *tehôm,* the deep.

[13]*Creation Epic,* tablet 5. Cf. James Pritchard, *op. cit.,* p. 68.

[14]Job's descriptions may best be understood in relation to the curiosity for exotic animals manifested by the Egyptians, and which reached a climax in the Ptolemaic period. See my *Manuel d'Archéologie Biblique,* vol. 2. (Paris, 1953) pp. 229, 307.

[15]J. Bonsirven, S. J., *Les idées juives au temps de Notre Seigneur* (Paris, 1934) pp. 40-43 and 52-54.

[16]Late Hellenistic speculation is the common source on which Christian and non-Christian authors are drawing.

[17]Mahmoud Mohtar Katirjoglou, *La Sagesse Coranique* (Paris, 1935) pp. 236-238.

[18]*Contra Arianos, or.* 3, PG 26:403.

[19]To these examples should perhaps be added the mysterious voices heard on the eve of the destruction of the Temple of Jerusalem, as reported by Fl. Josephus, *War* 6:299: "Let us go out of there!" Μεταβαίνωμεν ἐντεῦθεν.

[20]Quoting the powerful formula of St. Ignatius of Antioch: Λόγος ἀπὸ σιγῆς προελθών, *Epist. ad Magn.* 8, PG 5:669. Ignatius refers here to the Incarnation of the Word, but the same could be said of the creative Word of God.

[21]"The Wisdom embodied in Sophia is the design of God that preceded creation and called all celestial and earthly creatures forth from non-being into being, *out of the darkness of the night....* Sophia is what precedes the *days* of creation." Eugene Trubetskoi, *Icons: Theology in Color* (Crestwood, N. Y., 1973) p. 52.

CHAPTER V

[1]We need not enter here into the discussions of scholasticism, whether the original image did show a complete likeness, or would grow into likeness, or whether, once obliterated by sin, the likeness would be restored—all legitimate questions, but to which the Biblical text offers no immediate answer.

[2]As, for instance, the fragment on the four rivers (Gen 2:10-14), a curious blend of geography and folklore.

[3]"A garden in Eden." The name is derived from the Assyro-Babylonian *edinu,* dry land, steppe.

[4]Hebrew *tardêmah,* a supernaturally induced slumber. Cf. Gen 15:12; in both instances, the Greek has ἔκστασις. See also 1 Sam 26:12.

[5]The problem, whether Adam is the first human individual or man in general, as when we speak of "the twentieth-century man," has been blown out of proportion. The Semites are fond of designating a clan or race by the eponym. In a different perspective, the primacy of the universal idea over the individual reality in Platonic philosophy has strongly influenced patristic and mediaeval theology. The expression *Adam in genere humano* is commonly used in western scholasticism with the meaning: Adam, as type of the *genus* man.

[6]*Adv. haer.* 4:38, PG 7:1107-1108.

[7]*Adv. haer.* 5, *praef.,* PG 7:1120.

[8]This does not mean participation in the "Super-Essence," but in those essential aspects or active properties of the Divine Being which are communicable *ad extra;* cf. the ἐνέργειαι of Palamite theology.

[9]"Thou shalt surely die" (KJ), "You shall die" (RSV): weak rendering of the Hebrew *môth tâmûth,* "dying thou shalt die," "of death thou shalt die." Similar constructions are found in French folktales: *à manger mangeras-tu, à courir courras-tu.*

[10]Scene pictorially represented in a small relief on the southern wall of the Duomo in Florence, opposite the campanile of Giotto. The Virgin and the Angel Gabriel face each other on either side of a canopy, under which the dove of the Holy Spirit hovers with its wings extended. Mary has not stepped under the canopy; she is still wondering at the angel's words; she has not yet pronounced her *fiat.*

[11]Cf. E. Trubetskoi's suggestive remarks on the representation of the doubt of St. Joseph on some icons of the Nativity, *Icons: Theology in Color* (Crestwood, N. Y., 1973) p. 59.

[12]*Adv. haer.* 3:22, PG 7:957.

[13]Hugh of St. Victor (twelfth century) recensed them as the *sacramenta naturae,* prior to the "sacraments of the Law" and to the mysteries of the Christian Church.

[14]E. Dhorme saw in the Hebrew text a play on the double meaning of the Semitic root *sh-w-p,* to tramp, crush (cf. the Assyrian *shêpu,* foot) or to sight, to aim at (cf. in Arabic *shâfa, yashûf*). *La Bible de la Pleiade,* vol. 1 (Paris, 1956) p. 10-11.

[15]Conversely, the figures of Apollo and Orpheus as symbols of Christ in early catacomb paintings.

[16]*Second Apology* 10, PG 6:460.

[17]*Protreptikos* 5, PG 8:164-172.

[18]The bifurcation of western soteriology in the late Middle Ages and in classical Protestantism originates in an excessive contrasting of the two orders: on the one hand, an extrinsic gift of grace added to the natural powers of man and infused to the repentant sinner unto healing; in Protestantism, the total depravity of a creature which is not healed, but can only be forgiven through the atoning work of Christ.

CHAPTER VI

[1]"Sur quelques symboles de Iahvé," in *Mélanges Syriens offerts à Monsieur René Dussaud* (Paris, 1939) pp. 101-106. See my *Manuel d'Archéologie Biblique,* vol. 2. (Paris, 1953) p. 340.

[2]This route of the Aramaean tribes, which cattle men prefer to the direct crossing through the steppe, has been appropriately described in modern times as the "Fertile Crescent."

[3]Explained at a later date by means of an artificial etymology: *ab hamôn,* "father of a multitude," generally retained in patristic allegories.

[4]The well, originally dug out of the native rock and whose upper courses of masonry were added on account of the gradual raising of the terrain, is being used by the Greek monks, guardians of the church commemorating the meeting of Jesus and the Samaritan woman, near the village of Balata.

[5]The site is marked by the ruins of what seems to have been a monastic foundation. Cf. F. M. Abel, *Géographie de la Palestine,* vol. 2, p. 270.

[6]Mount Môriyyah is idendified by 2 Chr 3:1 with the northern hill of Jerusalem, upon which the Temple was built.

[7]"Legend" is not synonymous with "fiction"; it means rather a narrative, fictitious or real, destined to be read or proclaimed publicly.

[8]The entire fourteenth chapter seems to make use of an ancient source independent from the three "documents" regarded by the critics as the main sources of the Book of Genesis.

[9]The story supposes that the Dead Sea did not exist. Cf. Gen 13:10, where the southern part of the Jordan rift is described as a "garden of Yahweh."

[10]In the stories of Beersheba, God is called *El-'Olâm,* in the versions Θεὸς αἰώνιος, *Deus aeternus,* the Everlasting God. *'Olâm* is in reality a broader concept, expressing universality of time and space. Cf. the first *surat* of the Quran, where Allah is addressed as *Rab il-'alamîn,* "Lord of the worlds."

CHAPTER VII

[1]A political and cultural survey of the Near and Middle East in the time of Moses, and of the events of the exodus and of the march toward Canaan, is found in John Bright, *A History of Israel* (Philadelphia, 1959) pp. 97-127. The problem of the formation of the Pentateuch is discussed by Artur Weiser, *The Old Testament: Its Formation and Development* (New York, 1961) p. 70 ff.

[2]The pharaoh of the oppression seems to have been Ramses II (1301-1234 B.C.). The date generally favored for the flight of the Israelites is the latter half of the thirteenth century B.C. (between 1250 and 1230).

[3]Whether across ancient lagoons at the northern end of the Gulf of Suez, or in the region of the Bitter Lakes.

[4]I see no compelling reason for rejecting the traditional location of Mount Sinai. The alternatives proposed are based on tenuous clues which do not compare with the bulk of evidence in favor of the generally accepted site, and show an almost exclusive concern with modern theories on strategy and logistics, of a doubtful applicability to the case of Moses and his people.

[5]We need not enter here into the history of that hypothetical vocalization of the consonantal Hebrew text.

[6]*Cent. de caritate* 3:99, PG 90:1048.

[7]See above, chapter 6, note 1.

[8]*Paed.* 2:79, PG 8:488.

[9]The Simhat Torah is a post-exilic addition to the cluster of celebrations following *Sukkoth*, the great autumn festival, which tended to reduce the importance of *Shabû'oth* (Pentecost) as a memorial of the Sinaitic alliance.

[10]The Hebrew noun *Torah,* the Law, is derived from the verbal root *y-r-h,* to teach, to instruct.

[11]Elisha was credited with a similar miracle, when he cured the water of the spring of Jericho (2 Ki 2:19-22).

[12]Hellenistic Judaism attributes to a revelation of Divine Wisdom the miracle of the water from the rock (Wis 11:4; cf. Philo, *Comm. on Deut.* 8:15); this may be the source of St. Paul's exegesis, via the multiple equation Wisdom = Logos = Christ.

[13]Origen, *Hom. in Num.* 7:2, PG 12:613. Any attempt at desacralizing radically the institution of the Eucharist is bound to miss the point of the Gospel narratives, and any theology that rejects, or refuses to take into consideration the experience of the altar under pretense of transcending tradition or culture, or of accommodating it to the mood of the time or the particulars of a given denomination, is equally doomed to failure.

[14]We quote from the English translation of the *Haggadah* by Cecil Roth (London, 1934).

[15]The date of the Last Supper and its relation to the Passover of the Jews have been the object of many recent studies on the part of Christian scholars. No consensus was reached on the question of whether the Eucharist was instituted within the framework of the *sêder* meal, or after the *sêder*.

See V. Kesich, *The Gospel Image of Christ* (Crestwood, N. Y., 1972) pp. 56-60 and notes.

[16]There are many instances of this phenomenon of liturgical "conflation." Thus, the Feast of Weeks (*shabû'oth*), originally a harvest festival, fifty days after the apparition of the first ears of wheat, was supplemented with the memorial of the giving of the Law on Mount Sinai. Its counterpart in Christianity is Pentecost.

CHAPTER VIII

[1]The historical survey and the chronological tables which I drew for the *Oxford Bible*, respectively p. 1517 and p. 1532 ff, although starting from a lower, and more likely, date for the migration of Abraham, does not materially alter the picture.

[2]See my note and chronological chart in the *Interpreter's Bible*, vol. 1, p. 145.

[3]The appellation "Hexateuch" or even "Heptateuch" for the five Books of Moses, plus, respectively, Joshua and Judges, can be justified on these premises.

[4]An outstanding example is Jerusalem, which David conquered toward 1000 B.C. over the clan of the Jebusites, more than two hundred years after the invasion of Palestine by Joshua.

[5]The "Judges," in Hebrew *shophetim,* the title given to the magistrates of the Phoenician colonies in western Mediterranean lands. In Israel, the office of *shophêt* is not permanent, but pro tempore, as the circumstances demand.

[6]Critics tend to regard the "royalist" source as primitive. The satire of Judges 9:1-6 fits conditions that prevailed under Solomon and his successors and were stigmatized by the prophets.

[7]The Books of Chronicles (Paralipomena) reflect the traditions of the Temple scribes, and interpret the history of the kings of Judah from the special point of view of the Jerusalem priesthood.

[8]*Ostraca,* the technical name given to potsherds used as labels or short notes and inscribed with ink and a reed pen.

[9]Founders of dynasties and usurpers in the kingdom of Israel: Jeroboam, Baasha, Zimri (7 days), Omri, Jehu, Shallum (1 month), Pekah, Hosheah.

[10]Hezekiah's preparatives were regarded by Isaiah as indifferent measures, which a lack of trust in God would render futile (Is 22:9-11).

[11]Facsimile in the *Interpreter's Bible*, vol. 1, p. 164, n° 39.

[12]The *Qubbet es-Sakhra,* improperly called "Mosque of Omar," covers the rock on which the altar of burnt-offerings had stood. The memory of Solomon is preserved by the popular denomination *Istablât Suleiman,* "Stables of Solomon," given to the substructions of the mosque *el-'Aksa* at the southern end of the *Haram esh-Sherif,* a Holy Place of Islam, together with Mecca and Medina.

[13]The interdiction of trespassing was engraved on marble tables. Cf. my *Manuel d'Archéologie Biblique*, vol. 2 (Paris, 1953) p. 451f.

[14]The title of Psalm 72 attributes it to Solomon. On the nature and value of these notations, see chapter 12.

[15]Ps 110 is attributed to David. On the theme of the suffering messiah, see chapter 10.

CHAPTER IX

[1]This chapter and the following two incorporate the substance of a paper presented by the author at the Interorthodox Center in Athens. It appeared in the following: Εἰσηγήσεις Α΄ Ὀρθοδόξου Ἑρμηνευτικοῦ Συνεδρίου, 17-21 Μαΐου, 1972 (Ἀθῆναι, 1973); and *St. Vladimir's Theological Quarterly* 16 (1972).

[2]The passive meaning seems primitive, as in nouns of the same formation. The cognate verb is used only in derivate forms: *nibbâ'*, to be seized by a spirit of prophecy; *hithnabbî*, to act as a *nâbî'*.

[3]Also *hôzéh*, the "gazer."

[4]*Praefatio in Isaiam, ad Paulam et Eustochium.*

[5]According to Thiele's chronology of the Hebrew kingdoms, which is thus far the most satisfactory.

[6]It is generally agreed that the Book of Isaiah is composed of several collections: (1) a collection of Isaiah's own oracles (eighth century B.C.); (2) fragments and prophecies relating to the Babylonian exile and announcing the imminent intervention of Cyrus; (3) a collection of various post-exilic oracles. Allowance should be made for several fragments incorporated in what appears to be a wrong context. The final redactor was keenly aware of the development of a unique messianic theme which gives unity to his compilation and justifies to some extent the traditional ascription to Isaiah and his disciples.

[7]See above, note 4.

[8]"Shut their eyes *lest* they see" (Is 6:10); Hebrew *pén*, Greek μήποτε. God's prophetic warnings are a blessing to those who are disposed to receive them and repent. Otherwise they are a curse, inasmuch as the unrepentent sinner, by rejecting God's appeal, is, *ipso facto*, confirmed in his own blindness and obstinacy. See above, ch. 3, note 6.

[9]Prophetic names, like Immanuel, "God with us"; *Shear yashûb*, "A remnant shall return"; *Maher shalal hash baz*, "Prompt plunder, ready loot," are deemed effective of what they signify in much the same manner as an acted prophecy is believed to start an irreversible course of action.

[10]*In Isaiam* 7, PG 56:84.

[11]*In Isaiam* 7, PG 81:276.

[12]*Iliad* 2:513-514: Astyochè, παρθένος αἰδοίη, gave sons to Arès, who visited her in secret. Sophocles, *Trachiniai* 1219 ff: Hyllos shall take to himself the maiden (παρθένος) Iolè, his father's concubine.

[13]Cf. my essay on "Critical Exegesis and Traditional Hermeneutics," in *St. Vladimir's Theological Quarterly* 16 (1972), p. 110 and note 5, or in the acts of the Interorthodox Conference of Hermeneutics (see above, note 1).

[14]Rather than: *a* virgin (KJ and RSV).

[15]The RSV, following the Hebrew, reads: "Wonderful counselor" (without comma). The Greek had an obviously different prototype: "And his name shall be called: messenger of the Great Council, μεγάλης βουλῆς ἄγγελος."

[16]If, as it is very probable, the young king bearer of the wonderful names is the same person as Immanuel, then the oracle in 9:27 is not the giving of a sign for the contemporaries of Isaiah, as in the prophecy of the *'almah,* or the announcement of a recovery from imminent disasters, as in the oracle of the names, but a prophecy the accomplishment of which will take place in an indefinite, remote future.

[17]"He shall breathe," Hebrew *harihô,* as in the expression: "breathing honesty."

[18]These expressions are borrowed from the spiritual opuscules of Bonaventure (Bonaventura da Fidanza), *Itinerarium mentis ad Deum* (1259), and *De plantatione paradisi* (1270).

CHAPTER X

[1]"I have taken thee. . ." In the future in Greek: "I shall take thy hand and strengthen thee," ἐνισχύσω σε. In Hebrew, "I have formed thee," root *'-s-r,* to form, to model, as in Gen. 2:7.

[2]E. Dhorme, *La Bible de la Pléiade,* vol. 2 (Paris, 1959) p. 172, note 3. The words which make difficulty should not be regarded as an interpolation. They are attested unanimously by the massoretic Hebrew, Qumran, and the versions.

[3]"At seeing thee" (Hebrew, LXX and Vulgate). A "difficult" lection, however preferable to the "easy" correction: "at seeing him" (Targum and Syriac).

[4]In other words, the Servant was regarded as a leper.

[5]"His destiny." Hebrew *dôrô,* which the versions have translated by "his generation" (γενεάν), *generationem.* Dhorme, *op. cit.,* p. 189, note 8, observes that the original meaning of the word *dôr* is "circuit," "cycle"; by derivation, when speaking of men, their life-cycle. Here, the destiny of the Servant; in colloquial English, the "turn" his life has taken.

[6]"The rich," in the collective sense. A difficult lection, but well attested. The prophets repeatedly denounce the insolent riches of cities like Tyre and Babylon. The general meaning is that the Servant will be buried among sinners and unbelievers.

[7]The word "light" is lacking in the Hebrew and in the Latin Vulgate, but is attested by the LXX and the Qumran texts.

[8]"My pledgee," Hebrew *meshullam,* participle *pu'al* of the root *sh-l-m.*

[9]Vincent and Abel, *Jérusalem: recherches de topographie, d'archéologie et d'histoire,* vol. 2 (Paris, 1926) p. 855 ff.

[10]The existence of a school of prophets in the tradition of Isaiah is a possibility, which might claim some support from Is 50:4 and 54:13.

[11]C. R. North, *The Suffering Servant in Deutero-Isaiah* (Oxford, 1948). Also H. H. Rowley, *The Servant of the Lord and Other Essays* (London, 1952).

[12]The words are of Orlinsky, in a different context.

[13]Quite recently, by H. Orlinsky, "The So-Called 'Servant of the Lord' and 'Suffering Servant' in Second Isaiah," *Studies on the Second Part of the Book of Isaiah, Suppl. to Vetus Testamentum* 14 (Leiden, 1967). In Acts 9:34, Philip asks of the Ethiopian eunuch who was reading from Isaiah 53: "Of whom does the prophet speak? Of himself, or of someone else?" This can be interpreted as an allusion to some ancient tradition identifying the Servant and the prophet. But is it not rather a mere rhetorical question begging for the answer: "Someone else, of course."?

[14]"My anointed." A metaphoric anointing, indicating that Cyrus will play a providential role, like, in a former century, Hazael of Damascus and Jehu of Samaria, both reported to have been "anointed" by Elijah (1 Ki 19:15-16).

[15]Theodoret, anxious to save the reading "Thou art my servant, Israel" (Is 49:3), had recourse to an ingenious explication: "Hear the words which the Lord of the Universe spoke to Christ the Master as a man, calling him Jacob and Israel according to his visible nature." *Graecorum affectionum curatio* 10, PG 83:1081.

[16]See above, note 8.

[17]*Hom in Exod.* 7:7, PG 12:547.

[18]H. Snaith, "Isaiah 40-66: A Study of the Teaching of the Second Isaiah and its Consequences," in *Studies on the Second Part of the Book of Isaiah, Suppl. to Vetus Testamentum* 14 (Leiden, 1967).

[19]This is hardly the place to discuss the sweeping statements and cavils of some independent critics on the subject. See Fr. R. Tournay's review of Orlinsky's essay, in *Revue Biblique* 75 (1968) p. 592.

[20]Professor Snaith, *op. cit.,* stresses the triumph earned by the labors of the Servant, but deliberately limits his interpretation to the horizon of the sixth century B.C., lest he be carried beyond the range of the historical method by the traditional-liturgical insights of the Christian Church.

CHAPTER XI

[1]"Who did point." Literally; cf. the panel of the Isenheim altar in the cloister of the Unterlinden at Colmar (Alsace).

[2]St. Cyril of Alexandria, *In Joannis Evangelium,* PG 73:69.

[3]At the latest, prior to the version of the Septuagint and the scrolls of Qumran.

[4]*La Bible de Jérusalem* (Paris, 1956). See the "Introduction aux prophètes," especially p. 1124 ff. in the American edition.

[5]The religion of the city gates is a common theme in antiquity. Cf. the Assyrian descriptions of the gates of Nineveh, Ezekiel's project of restoration of Jerusalem, and the vision of the heavenly Jerusalem in Rev 21:10ff.

[6]These words, taken out of context, have been abusively quoted in order to minimize or reject sacramentalism and the function of ritual in worship.

[7]Verse 14 (Hebrew): "the product of Egypt and the profit of Kush." Our translation follows the Targum.

[8]This oracle refers to the messianic age, as was understood by the patristic and liturgical tradition. An allusion to Yahvistic cults in the Diaspora, for instance to the Temple at Elephantine in Upper Egypt or at Leontopolis in the Delta, is rather improbable.

[9]Zechariah's prophecy of the two shepherds, 11:3-17, which was certainly in the mind of Jesus, made a strong impression on the Evangelists, who saw in it a clear announcement of the rejection of the Jews, and who related the anecdote of the thirty pieces of silver, cast "into the treasury" (Hebrew) or "to the potter" (Targum), in connection with the episode of the remorse of Judas (Mt 27:3-10).

[10]The uprising of the Maccabees, of patriotic and religious inspiration, was without a morrow. The successors of Judas and Simon Maccabee could not withstand the dissolving influence of an all-pervading Hellenistic culture and the crafty politics of Rome.

[11]The two themes, the ruin of Jerusalem and the Parousia, are intertwined, and it is difficult to tell them apart, especially in Matthew and Mark.

[12]Athanasius, *Adv. Arian.* 3, PG 26:413. Basil, *Ad Amphil.*, PG 32:880. Gregory Naz., *Or.* 30:15, PG 36:124. Chrysostom, *In Matt. hom.* 77:1, PG 58:702.

CHAPTER XII

[1]Critical edition in *Sources Chrétiennes*, 2, PG 8:52.

[2]This is a matter of critical judgment. There has been a tendency to discount the attribution of the greater number of psalms to David. The pendulum now seems to swing back the other way, and to give to the traditional position the benefit of presumption.

[3]Similar indications, usually derived from the tunes of the Scottish Psalter, are found in modern Protestant hymnals.

[4]Their names are found in the genealogical tables of the Levites (1 Chr 25:1-7).

[5]*Praefatio in Psalmos:* "I know that some thought that the Psalter had been divided into five books. . . . However, following the authority of the Hebrews, and above all of the apostles, who always speak of 'the Book of Psalms,' we claim it to be one single volume."

[6]The Mishnah and the Talmud attribute to Ezra the final compilation of the Psalter.

[7]On the use of the Psalter in the Synagogue and in the Christian churches, see John A. Lamb, *The Psalms in Christian Worship* (London, 1962).

[8]*Hê-hag.* Cf. the Arabic *hadj,* the pilgrimage, of which the essential rite is the circuit around the "House of Allah."

[9]Feast on November 3/16. "Anniversary of the Dedication of the church that is at Lydda" (notice of the *Sluzhebnik*).

[10]Most likely a reference to an ancient oil well; cf. the reports of the Greek and Roman geographers, and the "Greek fire" in the Middle Ages.

[11]The "Feast of weeks" (*Shebû'oth*), viz. seven weeks *plus* one day: the fiftieth day after Passover (Pentecost). In the course of time, this feast had declined, several of its features being transferred to the autumnal feast of *Sukkoth*. From the Maccabaean period onward, the three popular festivals were Passover, *Sukkoth,* and the *Hanukkah* (Dedication of the Temple).

[12]They form the eighteenth *kathisma* in Byzantine usage. Under the name *Psalmi Graduales,* they were prescribed by Latin Breviaries in connection with the votive office of the Virgin Mary on Saturdays.

[13]Seven psalms have been singled out by the Latin liturgies under the title *Psalmi poenitentiales,* viz. Ps 6, 32, 38, 51, 102, 130, 143.

[14]Drawn from Psalm 130, a pilgrim song of confident hope. It is one of the seven *Psalmi poenitentiales* of the Latin liturgies, which use it profusely in the services for the dead. It is associated almost exclusively (and wrongly), by popular imagination, with death, funerals and tombstone inscriptions: *"de profundis."*

[15]"Sacred meals," viz. ritual meals following votive sacrifices, *shelâmim,* in which a portion of the victim was shared by the persons who offered them.

[16]*Shĕ'ol,* etymology uncertain: the place of the dead. *'Abaddon,* from the verbal root *'abad,* to perish, to waste away.

CHAPTER XIII

[1]Catholic editions of the English Bible print the historical books of the post-exilic and intertestamentary periods immediately after Kings and Chronicles.

[2]Cf. the radical exegesis of the early decades of the twentieth century, pitching the moral Yahvism of the prophets against the legalism of Temple worship, under pretense of upholding the cult "in spirit and in truth."

[3]A competent theological evaluation of the Sapiential Books is found in Gerhard von \Rad, *Wisdom in Israel* (Nashville, 1972).

[4]On the personnel of the royal chancery, see my *Manuel d'Archéologie Biblique,* vol. 2 (Paris, 1953) p. 61. Similarities between the sayings of

the Book of Proverbs and the sentences of the scribe Amenemhopé (ninth-sixth century B.C.), support the thesis of the Egyptian origin of the Solomonic bureaucracy.

[5]A literary device employed in several psalms, for instance Ps 37, 111-112, 119, and in the Lamentations, by which the initial letter of each verse, stich, or stanza of a poetic composition follows the order of the alphabet.

[6]The numerical pattern has been used repeatedly by some prophets, for instance Amos, ch. 1.

[7]The introduction, ch. 1-9, is certainly post-exilic. The final compilation is generally dated from the fifth century B.C. at the earliest.

[8]Ἐνέργεια, as St. Maximos the Confessor and St. Gregory Palamas have defined this term.

[9]Quoting from Pindar, *Pythian Ode* 8:95-97.

[10]Necromancy was strictly forbidden by the Law, cf. Lev 19:31; 20:6, 27; Deut 18:11, but it continued to be practiced in Israel, cf. 1 Sam 28:8-25, 2 Ki 21:6, Is 8:19.

[11]The latter anecdote may be an amplified version of Elijah's miracle by the redactor of the Elisha stories.

[12]The translation of these terms by "body" and "soul" is misleading. It reads back into the Old Testament a dichotomy of Greek origin.

[13]In Hebrew: "my *go'êl*," a term of law: he who shall answer for me in justice or demand satisfaction on my behalf.

[14]*Eloah:* poetic for *Elohim*, God.

[15]This is being done by a number of modern theologians who have little use for the categories of Hellenism, the traditionalism of the "Old Church," and who neglect or reject the deuterocanonical writings.